UCLAAnderson
School of Management

Judy D. Olian
Dean and John E. Anderson Chair in Management

Tel (310) 825-7982 Fax (310) 206-2073
judy.olian@anderson.ucla.edu

John Wooden is a monumental figure in American sports, yet his legacy of leadership transcends athletics and spans generations. Coach Wooden instills in others a sense of pride, a commitment to ethics and a respect for teamwork. These fundamental principles translate readily from the sports arena to business, management and leadership.

The UCLA Anderson School of Management is privileged to partner with the Coach in creating the John Wooden Global Leadership Program, based upon his fundamental principles. We established this program because Coach Wooden's philosophy and methodology of leadership and team building – character-based, practical, and values driven – are as relevant and applicable today, as ever. We are proud to partner with Coach Wooden in creating an academic home for his teachings on leadership and management.

Although John Wooden gained fame at UCLA as an illustrious basketball coach, his leadership values, professional and personal behavior are as applicable in business. Team building in any context – especially in today's hyper-competitive and fast changing environment – is difficult. That Coach Wooden was able to achieve such consistent successes at the highest levels over his forty year career is a tribute to the robustness of his ideas.

A significant component of this new program was the inauguration of the UCLA Anderson / John Wooden Global Leadership Award, which will be given annually to an outstanding individual who reflects the leadership values personified by Coach Wooden. In 2008, Howard Schultz, Chairman and CEO of Starbucks, received the first JWGL Award. In future years, UCLA Anderson will continue to celebrate the best in leadership. The John Wooden Global Leadership Program is an important ingredient of that overarching goal.

We are also very pleased that Steve Jamison, Coach Wooden's longtime collaborator and author on the coach's leadership philosophy, will serve as a consultant to the UCLA Anderson / John Wooden Global Leadership Program.

Judy D. Olian
Dean and John E. Anderson Chair in Management

110 Westwood Plaza, Mullin Management Commons
Suite F407 , Box 951481, Los Angeles, CA 90095-1481
www.anderson.ucla.edu

COACH WOODEN'S

LEADERSHIP GAME PLAN FOR SUCCESS

12 Lessons for Extraordinary Performance and Personal Excellence

JOHN WOODEN
AND STEVE JAMISON

McGraw-Hill

NEW YORK   CHICAGO   SAN FRANCISCO
LISBON   LONDON   MADRID   MEXICO CITY   MILAN
NEW DELHI   SAN JUAN   SEOUL   SINGAPORE
SYDNEY   TORONTO

6 7 8 9 0   DOC/DOC   1 3

MHID   0-07-162614-X
ISBN 978-0-07-162614-9

Interior design by Lee Fukui and Mauna Eichner

McGraw-Hill books are available at special quantity discounts to use as
premiums and sales promotions, or for use in corporate training pro-
grams. To contact a representative please visit the Contact Us pages at
www.mhprofessional.com.

Photocredits
Title page: ©Sports Illustrated/ Getty images
pp. xvi, 10 (right), 16 Purdue Sports Information Office/Special Collection
Library (Elmer Reynolds)
pp. 26, 118 Indiana State University Archives, Athletic Photograph Collection
pp. 1, 27, 29, 35, 71, 101, 103, 108, 112, 125, 129, 134, 138, 143, 152, 191,
213, 223 ASUCLA
p. 121, 148 *South Bend Tribune*
p. 273 Uncle Roy Stark

This book is printed on acid-free paper.

To Nell, whose love and support throughout these years has been my strength. And Nan and Jim whose strength through these years has been their love.

—JOHN WOODEN

*To Mary and Ev Edstrom, my parents.
And to Coach Wooden, my teacher and friend.*

—STEVE JAMISON

CONTENTS

GREETINGS
FROM COACH JOHN WOODEN

*Whether your team has talent to spare
or is spare on talent, a leader's goal
remains the same; namely, you must bring forth
the best from those with whom you work.*

Most leaders define winning as beating an opponent, gaining supremacy over the competition in the marketplace, achieving production or sales goals.

For any of these objectives to be met, talent must be present within your organization. A leader can't create a competitive team out of nothing; no coach can win consistently, and no leader can prevail in the marketplace without good material.

However, while you need talent to win, many leaders don't know how to win even with talent in their organization. Furthermore, we are frequently forced to compete when the talent match-up isn't in our favor. What then?

*When you're
through learning,
you're through.*

Over and over I have taught that we all have a certain potential, unique to each one of us. A unique potential also exists for every team. My responsibility as a leader—and yours—is to make the utmost effort to bring forth that potential. When this occurs, you have achieved success. Then, perhaps when circumstances come together, we may find that we are very competitive, perhaps even number 1.

It is my belief that when this occurs—being number 1, winning—it is simply a by-product of leadership that knows how to get the most out of a team that is very talented. Thus, for me the highest standard is success—the knowledge that you have made the effort to teach your team how to work together at their highest level.

And that, in my opinion, is the first goal of leadership— namely, getting the very best out of the people in your organization, whether they have talent to spare or are spare on talent.

Coach Wooden's Leadership Game Plan for Success seeks to offer details of how I went about bringing forth my own potential and that of our teams—striving to reach an uppermost level of our competency.

In some seasons the teams I taught were blessed with significant ability. Other years this was not the case. But in all years and with all levels of talent, my goal remained exactly the same, namely, to get the most out of what we had.

What I teach has stood me in good stead during nearly a half century in the competitive arena, and in spite of all of the changes we see around us, I believe it can be equally effective in the twenty-first century. Why? Because in many ways, the more things change, the more they stay the same.

And one of the things that has stayed the same is people— human nature hasn't changed.

Best wishes

John Wooden

BIOGRAPHY

John Wooden strides across twentieth-century sports in America in a singular manner—a preeminent and most revered coach, teacher, and leader. His UCLA basketball dynasty won 10 national March Madness championships, including seven in consecutive years. Under his leadership the UCLA Bruins had four perfect seasons and set the all-time record for consecutive victories: 88. Experts generally agree these records will stand forever.

The UCLA teams won 38 straight playoff games (a record) and appeared in the Final Four 12 times during a 14-year period (a record).

The past is for reference; the future for dreamers. The present moment is where you create success: make it a masterpiece.

During his 40-year coaching career, John Wooden had one losing season, his first. He taught at Dayton High School in Kentucky for 2 years; South Bend Central High School for 9 years; Indiana State Teachers College for 2 years; UCLA for 27 years. During that time his teams won over 80 percent of their games.

As a student-athlete at Purdue University, John Wooden was the nation's first three-time, all-consensus, All American and led the Boilermakers to a national championship.

Upon graduation from Purdue in 1932, the university president, Edward Elliot, awarded him the Big Ten Medal for Scholastic and Athletic Prowess.

Mr. Wooden was selected by ESPN as "The Greatest Coach of the 20th Century." In 2003 he received the nation's highest civilian honor, the Medal of Freedom Award, in ceremonies at the White House. According to *Sports Illustrated*, "There's never been a finer coach in American sports than John Wooden. Nor a finer man."

In 2008 the prestigious UCLA Anderson School of Management established the John Wooden Global Leadership Program. In coming years, the school will serve as the academic home for sharing the principles of Mr. Wooden's philosophy and methodology of leadership.

PREFACE

BY STEVE JAMISON

Coach Wooden's Leadership Game Plan for Success is a response to the great interest in and acceptance by the business community and academic world of two earlier publications: *Wooden on Leadership* (McGraw-Hill) and *The Essential Wooden* (McGraw-Hill). Those bestsellers introduced John Wooden's leadership concepts to a new and large corporate audience in America. Here we extend his teaching on leadership and offer a commonsense approach to understanding and incorporating his concepts.

The great coach, now 98 years old, reminds us that when it comes to leadership, teaching, and coaching there is no one right way, or "only way," but many ways. He offers his own lessons from his own experience with that in mind as well as the hope that you'll find some observations and directions that lend themselves to bringing out your best as a leader.

In large part John Wooden is self-taught. When he was coming up as a young man, there were no graduate courses in leadership, no gurus of management, no large section at the bookstore titled "Leadership and Management." You basically had to figure it out for yourself. And he did.

I believe to a large degree this still holds true. You have to pay attention to what's going on; you have to be a good listener and learner. As you'll see here, John Wooden was an astute listener and a voracious learner.

In the process he became an historic leader.

Just as John Wooden took the words and deeds of his father and mentors in new directions with creative applications, he hopes you will do the same with his body of teaching.

We've included questions that call for reflection and the creation of some straightforward steps on your part, but that's just to prime your pump. The real evaluation, introspection, and application of this book's substance in your leadership is up to you. The most important questions, the most valuable tasks you design as derived from Coach Wooden's philosophy and methodology will come from you.

For many years many people thought of John Wooden as a teacher of basketball only. Since he stepped away from active coaching following UCLA's tenth national championship, his ideas and example have become increasingly revered and taught by others outside of sports.

Most recently UCLA's Anderson School of Management established the John Wooden Global Leadership Program to promulgate his leadership philosophy—character-based— in its graduate program.

To paraphrase Ben Jonson's description of William Shakespeare (one of Coach Wooden's favorites), I would suggest the following: "The leadership concepts of John Wooden are not for an age, but for all time." And, in the eyes of many, including me, Coach Wooden is an all-time great leader.

TEN THINGS I MOST RESPECT ABOUT
* JOHN WOODEN *

1. John Wooden broke the color barrier.

In 1947 Coach Wooden's Indiana State Teachers College basketball team—the Sycamores—was offered a berth in the N.A.I.A. basketball tournament, one of the nation's first prominent college play-off events. The tournament, like others, excluded African Americans.

Clarence Walker, a nonstarter on the Sycamores team, was black. Without fanfare, John Wooden turned down the invitation because he refused to participate in segregation.

The following year Coach Wooden's team was again invited to play because of national attention being given his modern "racehorse" offense and the Sycamore's 27-7 record. Again, he turned down the invitation.

In response, N.A.I.A. officials quietly but quickly changed their racial policy and re-invited the Sycamores. This time Coach Wooden accepted and in the process broke the color barrier. Clarence Walker became the first black to play in a national basketball tournament for white colleges.

2. Ten national championships didn't change John Wooden.

His historic achievements at UCLA—creating perhaps the greatest dynasty in sports history—did not turn John Wooden's head. His tastes remained the same: favorite meal, Anderson's pea soup; favorite apparel, a blue cardigan sweater; favorite part of his job, conducting practice with his players in the gymnasium. Other than sharpening his skills and broadening his knowledge, John Wooden remained the same man while the records were being set— and after—as before the sports nation knew his name. Somehow, fame did not change him.

3. John Wooden treats people right.

Whether you're the boss or the busboy, a CEO or a secretary, John Wooden gives you his sincere attention. His father's advice guides him: "Never believe you're better than somebody else, Johnny, but always remember you're just as good as anybody." Just as good, but no better. In Coach's view, until he sees otherwise, every person he meets deserves to be treated with respect. And he does.

4. John Wooden practices "value-added" performance.

When asked to work for an hour, Mr. Wooden stays longer. When asked to donate a dollar, he gives more. Throughout his life John Wooden has gone beyond the minimum daily requirements both professionally and personally. He does the job and then some. Although he believes it is impossible to give more than 100 percent of oneself, he seems to do it.

5. John Wooden is savvy.

Over the decades he has become a keen student of human nature and is quick to spot ulterior motives, hidden agendas, and all the rest. Behind his cordial demeanor is someone who won't be fooled—with one caveat: Coach Wooden believes, "It is better to trust and be disappointed occasionally than to mistrust and be miserable all the time." He is comfortable being fooled on occasion if he gave his trust to someone who subsequently let him down.

6. John Wooden remembers his roots.

He grew up on a little farm near a little town in the center of America. John Wooden has never seen any reason to act in a manner contrary to what he learned in Centerton, Indiana. Manners matter, work counts, and when you say you'll do something you do it. Simple as that.

7. John Wooden is a master of productive criticism.

Being critical is a constant in coaching. John Wooden is a master at criticizing in a manner that brings improvement because he does not unintentionally create antagonism or resentment in the process. This was possible, in part, because at all times with all players he never got personal, never extended specific criticism to a general rebuke of the individual. His criticism—often very sharp—did not create a "mess" that had to be cleaned up later. When the issue was addressed and fixed, it was over. Time to move on. No hard feelings.

8. John Wooden is smart, in part, because he listens.

A conversation with Coach Wooden may include subjects as diverse as the Fifth Amendment, international politics, Shakespeare, rule changes in NCAA Division I basketball, movie stars, and more. The key word: conversation. He enjoys talking; he enjoys listening just as much. Perhaps this is because of an observation by his dad, Joshua Hugh Wooden: "You'll never know a thing that you didn't learn from somebody else." John Wooden knows you can't learn from somebody else if you're talking all the time.

9. John Wooden measures himself by a radical definition of success.

One of the winningest championship coaches in American history, John Wooden has never defined his ultimate success by victory. "Winning is very important," he observes. "Why else would we keep score?" There is, however, something even more important, a standard higher than the score. Coach Wooden hews to a definition of success that he places above winning, namely, "making the effort—

100 percent—to become the best you are capable of becoming." Few understand, but his standard of success is more difficult to achieve than merely winning. It is one of the reasons John Wooden became such a big winner.

10. John Wooden loves and has always been true to one woman.

"She was my sweetheart for 60 years and my dear wife for 53," he tells us. Nellie was his partner—co-coach—in raising their family, his confidant and one true love. When he lost her on the first day of spring, 1985, "I almost died from grief." Today he still grieves for his sweetheart.

ACKNOWLEDGMENTS

The Authors wish to thank the following for their great support:

Dean Judy Olian: UCLA/Anderson School of Management

Dr. Stephen Covey

Dan Guerrero, Director of Athletics, UCLA

Kim Edstrom: Executive Director: John Wooden Leadership Course

Julie Winter

Andy Serwer: *Fortune*; Managing Editor

Rich Karlgaard: *Forbes*; Editor and Publisher

Paul Asel and *Wharton Leadership Digest*

McDonalds Corporation and McDonalds All American Games

Bill Carlino: Editor-in-Chief; *Accounting Today*

General Mills Corporation

The 3 Amigos: Charlotte Bertling-Erland; John Russett; Rue Patel

Jim Wooden

Nan Wooden Muehlhausen

Mary Jean Edstrom

Sophia's Valley Inn

VIPs

PART I

ORIGINS OF LEADERSHIP

A COMPASS FOR CORE VALUES

THE ORIGIN OF MY LEADERSHIP

My Compass For Core Values | by John Wooden

The best man I've ever known is my father, Joshua Hugh Wooden. He was also my greatest teacher. What Dad taught me, and how he taught it, had a most profound impact on what I did professionally.

In style and substance, much of what I taught in 40 years as a leader and coach can be traced back in some manner to his own teaching, his own example back on our farm in Centerton, Indiana.

My father had a commonsense kind of wisdom. A man of few words, when Joshua Hugh Wooden said something, he really said something.

My dad

Johnny, never cease trying to be the best you can be.

Four of his important guiding principles have been a compass for me in my years of teaching, important words and deeds I have tried to live by and teach others. Dad's principles, the points on his compass, had to do with ethics and attitude. I didn't know it at the time, but he was giving me what is at the core of strong leadership.

Try your hardest; make the effort; do your best.

A MESSAGE REPEATED OFTEN
BY JOSHUA HUGH WOODEN.

Ethics and Attitude

*Be more concerned with your character than
with your reputation. Character is what you really are.
Reputation is what people say you are.
Character is more important.*

*I am not what
I ought to be,
Not what I
want to be,
Not what I
am going to be,
But I'm thankful
that I am
better than I
used to be.*

John Wooden's leadership was "character-based" before the word was invented. His philosophy and methodology are grounded in straightforward attitudes, values, and principles taught by his father, Joshua Hugh Wooden. The genesis of John Wooden's "character-based" leadership is traced back to what he learned growing up on a small farm in Centerton, Indiana, in the 1920s. Here are the four navigation points on John Wooden's compass for life and leadership that he learned from his father:

1. THE GOLDEN RULE

According to John Wooden, "My father came as close to living the Golden Rule as anyone I have ever known."

The Wooden family farmhouse, Centerton, Indiana

There is a choice you have to make in
everything you do. So keep in mind that in the end
the choice you make makes you.

Coach John Wooden, Dayton (KY) High School, 1932

The example of Joshua Hugh Wooden's "living the Golden Rule" made a profound and lasting impression on the future teacher and coach. Consciously and unconsciously "treating others as you would have them treat you" became a near-inviolable tenet of John Wooden's leadership. It is *the first navigation point* on his compass of character-based leadership.

2. DAD'S TWO SETS OF THREES

Joshua Hugh Wooden repeatedly reminded his four sons—Maurice ("Cat"), Johnny, Dan, and Bill—of his two lists (sets) with instructions offering directives on ethics and attitude. The first set gave three instructions on integrity:

1. Never lie.

2. Never cheat.

3. Never steal.

The second set gave three suggestions on how to face adversity:

1. Don't whine.

2. Don't complain.

3. Don't make excuses.

Joshua Wooden and sons Billy, Dan, Johnny, and "Cat"

Joshua Hugh Wooden's Two Sets of Threes offer straight-forward advice; simple to understand, not so simple to abide by. They became *the second navigation point* on John Wooden's compass.

3. The Caution against Comparisons

Throughout his early years, the future coach was told by his father to do the following when it came to the competition and comparing himself to others: "Johnny, don't worry about being better than somebody else, but never cease trying to be the best *you* can be. You have control over that. Not the other." Eventually this advice would spur him to

> *Strive to accomplish the very best that you are capable of. Nothing less than your best effort will suffice. You may fool others, but you can never fool yourself. Self-satisfaction will come from the knowledge that you left no stone unturned in an effort to accomplish everything possible under the circumstances.*

redefine success in a manner that was radical. In the process, John Wooden largely freed himself from the judgment of outsiders. What mattered most was not how he fared in comparison to others, but how close he came to his father's advice: ceaseless effort in bringing forth his own potential. He allowed no one, not even the scoreboard, to tell him whether or not he had succeeded in achieving this. John Wooden became the only judge of his success that mattered to John Wooden. It is *the third navigation point.*

4. DAD'S SEVEN-POINT CREED

Upon graduation from a country school in Centerton, Indiana, John Wooden received a gift from his father: a two-dollar bill. More important, Joshua Hugh Wooden also gave his son a 3 x 5 card on which he had written what would become *the fourth navigation point*:

"Seven Suggestions to Follow"

1. Be true to yourself.

2. Help others.

3. Make each day your masterpiece.

4. Drink deeply from good books—including the Good Book.

5. Make friendship a fine art.

6. Build a shelter against a rainy day.

7. Pray for guidance, count and give thanks for your blessings every day.

SUMMARY

John Wooden is frequently cited as an example of a values-based leader, one whose positive and productive principles were intrinsically woven into his system. What he did on the court reflected who he was off the court. Who he was, and is, is a direct reflection of the basic teachings of his father, Joshua Hugh Wooden, and the compass he gave his son for navigating through life and leadership.

THE EVOLUTION OF MY LEADERSHIP

Ability may get you to the top,
but it takes character to stay there.

MY THREE GREAT MENTORS | by John Wooden

Three mentors had a profound influence on my leadership in both style and substance. Each man contributed significantly to what I embraced and taught as a coach.

While my father provided the foundation for my philosophy, the compass for ethics and attitude, these three mentors—all coaches—were crucial to its evolution. Obviously, I worked hard to improve my teaching as the years went on, increasing my self-control, patience, and more, but these men had a tremendous impact on what I taught and how I taught it.

Earl Warriner   **Glenn Curtis**   **Ward "Piggy" Lambert**

Before you can be a good leader,
you must be a good follower.

DEFINE THE STAR, TEACH DETAILS, EXTEND YOUR FAMILY

Define the Star

EARL WARRINER: THE STAR OF THE TEAM IS THE TEAM

John Wooden attended Centerton Grade School—one mile down a dirt road from the family farm. The principal and basketball coach of the school, Mr. Earl Warriner, taught one of the strongest lessons in team building that John Wooden ever learned; namely, no single person is more important than the team.

A leader must accomplish the difficult task of getting those on the team to believe that "we" supersedes "me."

"The star"

Who is the star of the team?

If a grade school basketball team could have a "star," Joshua Hugh Wooden's son Johnny was it; the "gunner" more likely to make a basket than not. One day he forgot his basketball jersey and tried to use his position as "most important player" to force a teammate to run back to the Wooden farm and fetch it for him before the game started.

Coach Warriner would not allow it. Instead, he benched young Wooden and kept him on the bench even though it meant losing the game. "Some things are more important than the score, Johnny," was his explanation. He was telling the young "star" that the star of the team is the whole team.

> *A Simple Recipe for Teamwork:*
> *It is amazing how much we can accomplish if no one cares who gets the credit.*

John Wooden never forgot this message, and its application was seen on all of his teams, including those that won 10 national championships.

As a coach, it was a fundamental principle of his philosophy. Even with superstars such as Kareem Abdul-Jabbar or Bill Walton, the *team* was the star.

Teach Details

GLENN CURTIS: TEACH DETAILS

Glenn Curtis, John Wooden's coach at Martinsville High School, stressed the importance of basics—fundamentals—and how to teach them. Coach Curtis would break the mechanics of basketball down into small and separate pieces.

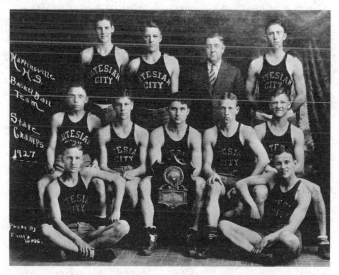

Indiana High School basketball champions, 1927.
Johnny Wooden, second row, second from right.

13

The players would practice each individual element until it was perfected. Then they would put the pieces back together into a whole under the direction of Coach Curtis.

This applied to running routes on plays, the mechanics of passing, shooting, rebounding, and everything else. Often practice consisted of drills without the basketball.

In fact, there are no "big" things, only an accumulation of little things done well.

Later, Coach Wooden took this approach much farther in his own system—eventually even showing players how to correctly put on socks and lace and tie shoelaces on sneakers to prevent blisters.

Basics—details, fundamentals—are the underpinning of great performance in basketball or business. An organization will not achieve or sustain success when sloppiness in the execution of relevant details is permitted. John Wooden began learning how to squeeze sloppiness out of preparation and performance from Coach Curtis. He applied it most effectively in building the UCLA basketball dynasty.

Basics—details and fundamentals—are the underpinning of great performance in basketball or business.

Extend Your Family

WARD "PIGGY" LAMBERT:
YOUR TEAM IS YOUR EXTENDED FAMILY

Purdue University's Ward "Piggy" Lambert was "the most principled coach I have ever known," according to

John Wooden. Mr. Lambert's impact on his young guard—a three-time all-consensus All American—is profound.

As a mentor Coach Lambert taught many things in many ways. This included his "Big Three": Condition, Fundamentals, and Team Unity (later, they would be included in the heart of Coach Wooden's Pyramid of Success).

Successful leadership is not about being tough or soft, sensitive or assertive, but about a set of attributes. First and foremost is character.

Most important, John Wooden learned from Coach Lambert's example that the team becomes a leader's extended family. Time and again the great Purdue coach made decisions that were in the best interests of "his boys" even when fans and alumni opposed him.

When the Purdue Boilermakers—Big Ten champions—were invited to appear in a tournament at New York's Madison Square Garden, Coach Lambert turned it down because he believed the big city environment—commercialization, gambling, and other temptations—was not in the best interests of the players.

His care and concern for their welfare precluded putting them in a setting that he wouldn't condone for his own children.

For Coach Lambert, the team was truly his extended family. "Piggy" Lambert was stern, a taskmaster and a fiery competitor, but he loved his team even to the point of

Johnny Wooden and Purdue Coach "Piggy" Lambert

making decisions that caused him to be harshly criticized by outsiders. He stood up for "his boys" even when he had to stand alone. (A few years later, a gambling scandal at the New York tournament involving several college players proved Coach Lambert correct.)

The principled leadership of Ward "Piggy" Lambert was the model for what John Wooden set out to become as a coach.

He stood up for his team *even when*
he had to stand alone.

S U M M A R Y

An effective leader is forged by events, experience, observation, and education. All of this was true in John Wooden's own evolution in leadership, teaching, and coaching. However, the impact of Earl Warriner, Glenn Curtis, and Ward "Piggy" Lambert on his philosophy and methodology is surpassed only by that of his father, Joshua Hugh Wooden.

When he became a teacher of basketball, a leader of teams, much of what John Wooden tried to do was a direct reflection on what these mentors had taught while he had been their student.

C O M P A S S   C H E C K

✳ THE GOLDEN RULE ✳

Treat others as you would have them treat you.

- In today's business environment, is The Golden Rule applicable or naïve? Describe your perspective.

_____

_____

_____

_____

_____

_____

- Identify three leaders who embody The Golden Rule and three leaders who do not. Evaluate their effectiveness as it applies to "treating people right."

_____

_____

_____

_____

_____

_____

_____

_____

_____

- Everybody pays lip service to The Golden Rule. In what circumstance would you allow yourself to break "The Rule"? Explain your reasoning.

_____

_____

_____

_____

_____

_____

_____

_____

_____

✳ DAD'S TWO SETS OF THREES ✳

1. Never lie.
2. Never cheat.
3. Never steal.

1. Don't whine.
2. Don't complain.
3. Don't make excuses.

- What is the practical application of John Wooden's Two Sets of Threes in your own leadership?

_____

_____

_____

_____

_____

_____

_____

- How resolute are you in applying the first Set of Three?

_____

_____

_____

_____

_____

_____

- Describe your own response to adversity and setbacks. Is the second Set of Three worth including in your leadership? In what way?

_____

_____

_____

_____

_____

_____

_____

✳ THE CAUTION AGAINST COMPARISON ✳

"Johnny, don't worry about being better than somebody else, but never cease trying to be the best you can be. You have control over that. Not the other."

- Evaluate your need for approval from others. Does it have a positive or a negative impact? Describe how.

_____

_____

_____

_____

_____

_____

_____

- Whose opinion/approval matters most to you professionally? How does it help or hurt your effectiveness?

_____

_____

_____

_____

_____

_____

_____

_____

_____

- What drawback(s) may be a result of setting yourself up as the ultimate judge of your effort and performance?

_____

_____

_____

_____

_____

_____

_____

_____

_____

_____

✳ DAD'S SEVEN-POINT CREED ✳

What specific goal do you pledge to fulfill for each point of Dad's Seven-Point Creed? How will you achieve each goal?

1. Be true to yourself.

2. Help others.

3. Make each day your masterpiece.

4. Drink deeply from good books—including the Good Book.

5. Make friendship a fine art.

6. Build a shelter against a rainy day.

7. Pray for guidance, count and give thanks for your blessings every day.

My Seven Commitments

1. Be true to yourself.

_____

_____

_____

_____

_____

_____

_____

2. Help others

_____

_____

_____

_____

_____

_____

_____

_____

_____

_____

3. Make each day your masterpiece.

_____

_____

_____

_____

_____

_____

_____

_____

_____

_____

4. Drink deeply from good books—including the Good Book.

_____

_____

_____

_____

_____

_____

_____

_____

_____

_____

5. Make friendship a fine art.

_____

_____

_____

_____

_____

_____

_____

_____

_____

_____

6. Build a shelter against a rainy day.

_____

_____

_____

_____

_____

_____

_____

_____

_____

_____

7. Pray for guidance, count and give thanks for your blessings every day.

_____

_____

_____

_____

_____

_____

_____

_____

_____

✳ YOUR LEADERSHIP EVOLUTION ✳

Various people and events in your life have helped mold the person and leader you are.

- Describe the mentor(s) who has (have) most influenced you professionally. Be specific about what you learned and how it is being applied.

_____

_____

_____

_____

_____

_____

_____

_____

_____

_____

_____

_____

_____

_____

_____

_____

_____

_____

_____

- How do you teach the principle of "team comes first," that is, "we before me"?

_____

_____

_____

_____

_____

_____

_____

_____

- Give an example of how you or someone on your team exhibited a dedication to identifying and perfecting a relevant detail. Is this attitude common among team members?

_____

_____

_____

_____

_____

_____

_____

_____

_____

- What are your own personal navigation points?

_____

_____

_____

_____

_____

_____

_____

_____

_____

_____

_____

_____

_____

PART II

THE
PYRAMID
OF SUCCESS

*On the first day of practice, Coach Wooden told us,
"Don't worry about whether you're doing better than
the next guy. Just give me your best. That's all I ask."
I knew I could do that. He had given me
a new definition of success.*
—Rafer Johnson,
Olympic Gold Medal Winner, Decathlon;
UCLA Varsity, 1958–59

I don't care how tall you are.
I care how tall you play.

When my Pyramid of Success was featured on the cover of the *New York Times Magazine* following UCLA's ninth March Madness national championship, most readers were puzzled. Many asked, "What is this new thing? Where did it come from?" Well, it wasn't new, and it came from me.

As a first-year teacher in 1932 at Kentucky's Dayton High School, I immediately became greatly disturbed by the extreme pressure many parents placed on students in my English classes. Anything less than an "A" was often viewed as failure even if the student had worked hard and done their best.

Similarly, I was greatly irritated to hear a father complain about his son's secondary role on our basketball team when I knew it was often the best the young student-athlete could do. The father's reaction was unfair and unproductive. It's hard to describe my deep disappointment, even disgust, when I saw this happen time and time again.

I do not accept the notion that the score can make you a loser when you have done your best. It cannot. Nor can it make you a winner if you have done less than your best.

How would you feel if you'd worked hard, paid attention, done your best!—only to be called a loser by someone you respected? Regardless of age, many would simply quit trying. I did not want anyone under my supervision to ever quit trying to do their best. And few ever did.

> A leader must be what he wants the team to become. Your example counts most.

Personal experience had taught me that sometimes you're defeated even when you do your best. On those occasions when the UCLA Bruins prepared hard and played to their potential, I judged them as a success even when we were outscored, and told them so. Was there something more I could require of them beyond their best? No.

Searching for a Standard Higher than Merely Winning

Perhaps I was just trying to find a way to teach others what my father had taught me.

Thus, during the first months of teaching and coaching at Dayton High School, I decided to develop a self-grading system that was both fair and very productive—something beyond A's in the classroom or points scored in a game.

I remembered what Dad had told me, "Don't worry about being better than somebody else, but never cease trying to be the best you can be." I began thinking that success should be graded along the lines he described, by one's effort, by how hard you try to achieve your best, whether in the classroom, sports, or life.

About this same time I read a very insightful little poem that gave me additional and specific direction:

> AT GOD'S FOOTSTOOL TO CONFESS,
> A POOR SOUL KNELT AND BOWED HIS HEAD.
> "I FAILED," HE CRIED. THE MASTER SAID,
> "THOU DIDST THY BEST, THAT IS SUCCESS."

That poem summed it up for me: do your best, that is success. Thus, in 1934, after very careful consideration, I wrote down my new definition of success. It is the standard I asked those under my supervision to strive for most of all. To me it is the highest and hardest standard to achieve: *Success is peace of mind that is a direct result of self-satisfaction in knowing you made the effort to become the best that you are capable of becoming.*

In my opinion, this definition of success creates a profoundly more productive standard than merely aiming to "outscore" somebody or trying to be better than another. Most important of all, it puts success totally under your own control. No one can give it to you; no one can take it away. No one except you. And so I began teaching this new definition of success to English students, student-athletes, and anyone else who cared to listen.

However, something unintended occurred almost immediately. What began as a search for a self-grading system for those under my supervision became the standard for success I applied to myself—the specific manner in which I began grading myself in life and leadership.

A Guide to Success: My Blueprint

Don't judge yourself by what you've accomplished, but rather by what you could have accomplished given your ability.

Coach Wooden, Indiana Teachers College, 1947

Soon thereafter I recognized that only half of the problem had been addressed, namely, redefining success. As a teacher, I understood it was necessary to help those under my supervision know how to attain it; what each needed to do to achieve success as I had defined it.

That's when I began "constructing" the Pyramid of Success—identifying those personal qualities and values that I believe are intrinsic to making the total effort to reach your potential as a person, whether in leadership or as part of a team; what it takes to do your best.

I was about to create a blueprint of my own values in life and leadership. You might call them the characteristics and qualities of success.

*The Pyramid contains 15 personal qualities that
I believe are necessary to achieve success.*

Beginning in 1934, Mr. Wooden began evaluating and identifying personal characteristics that were prerequisites for achieving success as he defined it. What must you do to acquire the peace of mind that is a direct result of self-satisfaction from knowing you made the effort to become the best you are capable of becoming?

As a teaching tool, he chose a structure that represented durability, strength, and permanence: the pyramid. During the ensuing 14 years he carefully evaluated, selected, and placed in specific locations of his pyramid the 15 personal qualities—each represented as a specific block—he concluded were necessary for achieving success, both as a leader and as a member of a fully functioning organization. He completed the Pyramid of Success in 1948, shortly before leaving Indiana State Teachers College to become head basketball coach at UCLA. It was the first thing Coach Wooden tacked up on the wall of his office at 301 Kerckhoff Hall (see page 35).

> *Success is peace of mind, which is a direct result of self-satisfaction in knowing you made the effort to become the best you are capable of becoming.*

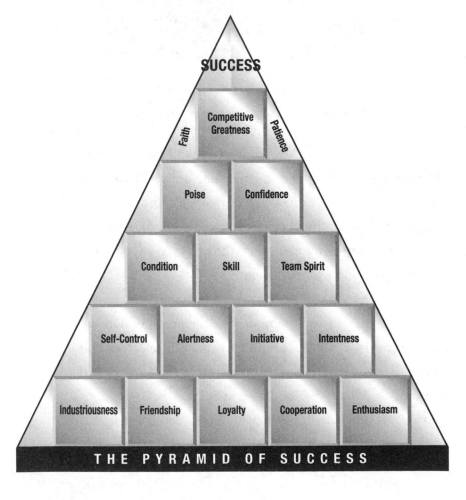

THE FOUNDATION
OF THE PYRAMID

Industriousness

THE HEIGHTS BY GREAT MEN REACHED AND KEPT,
WERE NOT ATTAINED BY SUDDEN FLIGHT.
BUT THEY, WHILE THEIR COMPANIONS SLEPT,
WERE TOILING UPWARD IN THE NIGHT.
— HENRY WADSWORTH LONGFELLOW

There is no trick, no easy way. Success travels in the company of very hard work. Work—hard physical labor—was a constant in John Wooden's childhood. There was no electricity or indoor plumbing. A healthy mule was considered a modern convenience.

He and his brothers quickly learned they'd go hungry if they didn't work. It was one of the first lessons in life he learned.

It was also the first block chosen—a cornerstone—for the Pyramid of Success. He called it "Industriousness" because of his accurate assessment that the word "work" had lost real meaning. For most people, it meant going through the motions, putting in time, enduring boredom. Mr. Wooden had something else in mind.

Industriousness, as he understood it, meant true work at your highest capacity; fully engaged, totally focused, and

37

Industriousness entails rising above the level of hard work.

completely absorbed; no clock-watching, no punching in and out, no going through the motions.

It is also something you cannot simply will yourself to do. The young teacher knew from personal experience that to reach Industriousness, a companion was necessary.

COACH WOODEN'S X'S AND O'S:

INDUSTRIOUSNESS

- You can work without Industriousness, but there is no Industriousness without work.

- Only you truly know if you're rising to a level beyond plain "hard work."

- "The heights . . ." attained by Tiger Woods, Cal Ripken, and Jack Nicklaus came from a will to win, coupled with their great will to work.

- It is not what you achieve that matters, but what you could have achieved. Industriousness is a key— irreplaceable—factor in becoming the best you can be.

Enthusiasm

WORK WITHOUT ENTHUSIASM IS JUST WORK. "JUST WORK" IS NOT ENOUGH.

Your energy and enjoyment, drive, and dedication will stimulate and greatly inspire others.

*As a leader, you must be filled with energy and eagerness,
joy and love for what you do. If you lack enthusiasm for
your job, you cannot perform to the best of your ability.
Industriousness is unattainable without Enthusiasm.*

At the family farm in Indiana, Johnny Wooden understood that plowing an acre of hard-baked dirt behind two
mules in 100-degree July heat was hard work. He also knew
that basketball practice as conducted by his high school
coach, Glenn Curtis, was even harder. In fact, it was physically and mentally more grueling than field work. And yet
John Wooden thrived on it. Why? Enthusiasm. His heart
was in it.

Industriousness is unattainable without Enthusiasm.
You must love what you do. If not, it is impossible to bring
out your best.

Enthusiasm was quickly chosen as the second cornerstone in Mr. Wooden's pyramid. Hard work is transformed
into Industriousness when joined with Enthusiasm. Together they catapult your performance engine to its highest
level. It is the most formidable engine of productivity.

Enthusiasm infuses and stimulates those you lead. The
energy and enjoyment, drive and dedication you exude is
emulated by those in your organization. According to
Coach Wooden, "In my opinion, these two qualities, Industriousness and Enthusiasm, are always present in those who
scale the heights—who achieve success as I define it."

Hard work is transformed into Industriousness
when joined with Enthusiasm.

COACH WOODEN'S X'S AND O'S:

ENTHUSIASM

- If your heart is not in your job, you cannot work to your full potential.

- A leader lacking Enthusiasm will infect the group with the same malady.

- Enthusiasm is the ignition switch. Turn it on and things start happening.

- If you lack Enthusiasm for your job, get out or at least recognize that you will never perform at your highest level.

"WORKING TOGETHER" BLOCKS WITHIN THE FOUNDATION

Between these potent foundation cornerstones of the Pyramid—Industriousness and Enthusiasm—Coach Wooden placed three "working together" blocks, personal qualities that are necessary because most of what we do involves interacting and working with others: Friendship, Loyalty, and Cooperation.

Friendship

THE TIME TO MAKE FRIENDS IS
BEFORE YOU NEED THEM.

Strive to build a team filled with camaraderie and respect: comrades-in-arms. Friendship in the context of leadership may strike you as a perplexing choice. Is it wise for leaders to become "friends" with those under their supervision? Could it undermine decision making when hard decisions are called for?

Coach Wooden suggests that we have friendships of different kinds: an acquaintance with whom we share an interest in politics or sports; another whose humor we enjoy; golfing, bowling, or fishing buddies. All are friends in different ways, but not in the way John Wooden means Friendship as it pertains to leadership and team building.

> *To make a friend, you must be a friend.*

The two characteristics of Friendship he identifies as of supreme importance for a leader to possess and instill in team members are the following: respect and camaraderie.

Camaraderie is a spirit of great goodwill that can exist between a leader and members of the team—comrades-in-arms. Think of how much you'll give when asked to do so by someone you respect; someone who is your comrade-in-arms. You'll give everything you've got. Those under your leadership will do the same if these qualities are offered by you.

*Seek to create a team that possesses camaraderie
and respect, whose members are "comrades-in-arms."
Where it exists, you'll find a tightly knit organization.*

COACH WOODEN'S X'S AND O'S:

FRIENDSHIP

- Respect, esteem, and camaraderie are characteristics of Friendship necessary for a high-performance team.

- Friendship is mutual, but the leader may have to be the first to prime the pump.

- Friendship includes others and is a powerful bonding agent.

- To paraphrase Abe Lincoln, "You destroy your adversary when you make him your friend."

Loyalty

THERE IS A DESTINY THAT MAKES US BROTHERS,
NONE GOES HIS WAY ALONE.
ALL THAT WE SEND OUT TO OTHERS,
COMES BACK INTO OUR OWN.
—EDWIN MARKHAM

Be true to yourself. Be true to those you lead. Loyalty creates trust. Loyalty is part of man's higher nature. It is also part of the nature of great teams and those who lead them.

The power of Loyalty is the reason Mr. Wooden placed it in the center of the Pyramid's foundation.

Is it possible to be a good leader without Loyalty to those on your team? Is it possible to be a good citizen without Loyalty to your country? The answer to both questions is the same. Of course not.

You must have the courage to be loyal to those you lead. This is not always easy. It starts, however, with Loyalty to yourself—your standards, your system, your values.

"To thine own self be true," Polonius advised his son, Laertes, in *Hamlet*. Coach Wooden extends that exhortation: "First, do not betray yourself. Second, do not betray those you lead." This is Loyalty.

> *Give loyalty and loyalty will be returned in abundance.*

People do not arrive at your organization's doorstep with Loyalty. It comes when they perceive that your concern for their interests and welfare goes beyond simply calculating what they can do for you or how you can use them to your advantage.

John Wooden believes that most people—the overwhelming majority—wish to be in an organization whose leadership cares about them; provides fairness and respect, dignity and consideration; and holds them to high standards.

Do this and you will find Loyalty in abundance from those you lead. You will find yourself in charge of an organization that will not waffle in the wind.

For that to happen, you must be true to yourself and your team. You must have Loyalty to those you lead. And when you give it, you will get it back from your team.

COACH WOODEN'S X'S AND O'S:

LOYALTY

- First, be true to yourself and your beliefs. Second, be true to your team.

- Respect is a prerequisite for Loyalty. You gain respect by giving respect.

- Just as you cannot be a good citizen without Loyalty to your country, neither can you be a good leader without Loyalty to your team.

- Let those you lead know you have sincere care, concern, and consideration for their welfare and you will generate great Loyalty from those on the team.

Cooperation

MAKE SURE THE PEOPLE YOU LEAD
FEEL THEY'RE WORKING WITH YOU, NOT FOR YOU.

Have the utmost concern for what's right rather than who's right. For this to occur, the final block of the pyramid's foundation must be present and active: Cooperation.

It is often difficult for a strong-willed leader to incorporate Cooperation because listening to others, evaluating, and embracing their opinions and creativity may seem to suggest uncertainty and doubt about your own judgment and convictions. The ego gets in the way of your eyes and ears. It's easy to get lost in your own tunnel vision.

Much can be accomplished by teamwork when no one is concerned about who gets credit.

An effective leader understands it is a sign of strength to welcome honest differences and new ideas from those on your team as well as others. Progress is difficult when you won't listen. Cooperation is impossible if we refuse to consider the merits of contrary opinions.

A dictator-style leader is all answers and no questions. The most effective leader incorporates the productive ideas and creativity of others, knowing it makes things work better. That's what John Wooden seeks: not just making something work, but making it work better and better.

Cooperation—the sharing of ideas, creativity, responsibilities, and tasks—is a priority of effective leadership. The only thing that is not shared is blame. A strong and secure leader accepts blame and gives the credit. A weak insecure leader gives blame and takes credit.

In basketball, one of the undervalued acts that Coach Wooden most values is the assist—helping a teammate score a basket. The assist in basketball epitomizes Cooperation.

The assist is valuable in all organizations—helping someone do their job better. It makes "scorers" out of everyone.

COACH WOODEN'S X'S AND O'S:

COOPERATION

- Much can be accomplished when nobody cares about who gets the credit.

- "One hand washes the other" is a good motto for a team seeking Cooperation.

- A strong team of field horses pulling in different directions will go nowhere.

- Seek the right way, not just having it your way.

THE SECOND TIER
OF THE PYRAMID

John Wooden chose four traits for the Pyramid's second tier that primarily involve control and direction of your mental and emotional faculties. The first quality block is the most explicit in this regard.

Self-Control

IF YOU DO YOUR BEST, NEVER LOSE YOUR TEMPER,
AND NEVER BE OUT-FOUGHT OR OUT-HUSTLED,
YOU'LL HAVE NOTHING TO WORRY ABOUT.

*Control of your organization begins with control of yourself.
Be disciplined.* Getting to the top, even once, is most difficult.
Staying there is arduous. Mr. Wooden understands that both
getting there and staying there present unique and formidable challenges. To do either requires great personal discipline: Self-Control.

Control of self is essential for consistency in leadership
and team performance. Coach Wooden views consistency as
a trademark of the true competitor and effective leader. This
is impossible to achieve without Self-Control.

Self-Control is necessary in all areas. The
choices you make in your personal life affect
your professional life. They are not separate. A
leader who lacks Self-Control outside the organization may lack it within the organization.

*Discipline
yourself and
others won't
need to.*

It starts with control of your emotions,
but it extends to having the resolve to resist the easy choice,
the expedient solution, and, at times, temptation in all its al-
luring forms.

Self-Control in little things becomes Self-Control in big
things. Coach Wooden prohibited profanity during practices

and games because it showed loss of control. In this small way—prohibiting profanity—he taught Self-Control that could be applied in other areas.

He told his teams that when they lose control, they make themselves vulnerable. The same is true for a leader who lacks Self-Control.

How did he teach Self-Control? In large part through his own example. His personal control of self became more and more effective over the course of many years. Ultimately it led an announcer to proclaim during a game, "Coach Wooden must be very upset. He just raised an eyebrow!"

COACH WOODEN'S X'S AND O'S:

SELF-CONTROL

- You cannot function responsibly and productively if you lack personal discipline—especially in the area of emotions. Anger is the most common culprit, but not the only one.

- Clear thinking is clouded by emotionalism.

- Self-Control creates consistency. Consistency is crucial to getting to the top and staying there.

- An undisciplined team is the best evidence of an undisciplined leader.

Alertness

NOTHING IS STATIC. EXPECT EACH DAY TO
BRING NEW THREAT AND OPPORTUNITY.

Constantly be aware and observing. Always seek to improve yourself and the team. Alertness—the ability to observe, absorb, and understand what's going on around you—is a critical component for the individual in charge, the leader, as well as those he leads.

You must constantly be awake, alive, and alert in evaluating yourself as well as the strengths and weaknesses of your organization and those of the competition.

> *Never be a spectator. Be in the fight at all times.*

In sports today we see instantaneous adjustments during play: video, photos, and spotters in the booths with binoculars providing immediate information on the game.

Should it be different with you and your team? The same sense of urgent observation—Alertness—must exist in you and be taught to those under your supervision.

A leader who is sluggish in recognizing what's going on will soon be going on without a job.

John Wooden's father liked to remind him that most of what he'd learn in life would come from others. That can happen only if you exhibit Alertness. A driver who's asleep at the wheel, not alert, will crash. The same happens to organizations whose leader does not exhibit Alertness. To learn, you must listen. Coach Wooden advises, "Don't just act like you're listening. Really listen. Good leaders are good listeners." It helps heighten Alertness.

Alertness must exist in you and be taught
to those under your supervision.

COACH WOODEN'S X'S AND O'S:

ALERTNESS

- Perfection doesn't exist. Thus, actively be alert and looking for imperfections in your team and your competition. It is there. Find it.

- Stick to your guns, but be open to change or you will be blindsided.

- Sports teams are constantly adjusting during a game to what the opponent does. Do the same.

- "Heads-up" leadership is alert to opportunity, threat, trends, and changes.

Initiative

FAILURE TO ACT IS OFTEN THE
BIGGEST FAILURE OF ALL.

Have the courage to make decisions and the willingness to risk failure. A basketball team that won't risk mistakes won't win many games. The same is true for any organization.

Fouls, errors, and mistakes are part of the competitive process in sports, business, and life. Not careless or sloppy mistakes, but those resulting from assertive action based on proper assessment of risk.

John Wooden's outstanding coach at Purdue, "Piggy" Lambert, summed it up like this: "The team that makes the most mistakes wins." He was talking about the next block of the pyramid: Initiative.

Many leaders instinctively behave like a young college basketball player who picks up three quick fouls in the first half and becomes cautious, tentative, and timid. A smart coach will sit this player on the bench before he can hurt the team.

The tentative business leader, however, stays in the contest, to the eventual detriment of the organization. Hesitancy brought on by fear of failure is not a characteristic of great leadership. Play to win rather than "not to lose."

Assume failure. Don't just stand around waiting to see if the ball goes in. Assume it won't. Get ready to respond quickly and correctly.

Coach Wooden instructed players, "Be quick, but don't hurry." Once you've decided on a course of action, take action. Initiate quickly, but not carelessly or in a fashion so hurried that a miscue is more likely.

Do not be afraid to fail. Use good judgment and then use Initiative. The leader who fears failure will often fail to act when action is required.

As a rule, Coach Wooden never benched or admonished a player who tried in an intelligent way to make something happen on the court—even when they failed. He did not want an environment where individuals were afraid to risk failure.

A leader must have Initiative—the courage to make decisions and the willingness to risk failure.

COACH WOODEN'S X'S AND O'S:

INITIATIVE

- Fear of failure is often the biggest failure of all.

- Have the courage to believe that you have nothing to fear when you've prepared your organization to the best of your ability.

- Respect all. Fear none.

- Never rebuke someone who makes a mistake after careful planning and proper preparation.

Intentness

IT'S NOT WHO STARTS THE GAME,

BUT WHO FINISHES IT.

Stay the course. When thwarted, try again—harder, smarter. Persevere relentlessly. Intentness is as important as any single block in John Wooden's Pyramid of Success. Without it you will falter, fade, and fall.

Mr. Wooden chose the word Intentness to suggest persistence and determination, fortitude and resolve. All of these traits are present in a great leader.

When Intentness exists within you, it also will exist within your organization. Unfortunately, the reverse is also true. Leaders lacking Intentness will find themselves leading teams intent on quitting, on finding the nearest exit.

Intentness also implies a firm resolve to stay the course over the long term rather than a burst of short-lived activity.

Intentness keeps you in the game even when others tell you the game is over. The game is over only when you, the leader, say so.

Never be satisfied. Work constantly to improve. Perfection is a goal that can never be reached, but it must be the objective. The uphill climb is slow, but the downhill road is fast.

Good things take time, usually lots of time. Achieving worthwhile goals requires Intentness. There are setbacks, losses, unexpected reversals, hardships, and bad luck. Does the fight continue? The team looks to you for their answer. Your answer is Intentness.

Industriousness and Enthusiasm are a powerful combination essential to Success. But the great force they produce must be constant and ongoing. They require Intentness.

Things achieved without effort are seldom worthwhile or long-lasting.

COACH WOODEN'S X'S AND O'S:

INTENTNESS

- Worthwhile goals often present formidable obstacles. It takes time to overcome serious challenges; accept it.

- Persevere! Change course, start over, alter methods, go over, around, or under. Do not give up.

- Nothing of consequence occurs without Intentness.

- Impatience can corrode and corrupt Intentness.

Condition

WHAT YOU DO AWAY FROM PRACTICE CAN TEAR DOWN ALL WE ACCOMPLISHED DURING PRACTICE.

Ability may get you to the top, but character keeps you there: mental, moral, and physical. Obviously physical conditioning is necessary—good health, vitality, and energy. However, in choosing Condition as a block in the heart of the Pyramid, Coach Wooden went beyond physical assets.

He understands that to achieve your leadership potential, you must also possess mental and moral strength. All three are present in this next block: Condition.

How does one attain moral Condition? John Wooden has prescribed a commonsense method for decades: Practice moderation and balance in all that you do.

Following a grueling basketball practice aimed, in part, at building up the players' physical strength, he would advise them of the following: "All we've worked so hard to accomplish on the court today can be torn down quickly, in a matter of minutes, if you make the wrong choices between now and our next practice."

He cautioned that when moderation and balance are lacking in their choices and subsequent actions, the team can be damaged. To help them understand what he meant—that ultimate responsibility for success lay with them—Coach Wooden occasionally posted the following reminder on the UCLA team bulletin board:

Be concerned with your preparation, not theirs; your execution, not theirs; your effort and desire, not theirs. Don't worry about them. Let them worry about you.

"There is a choice you have to make, in everything you do. So keep in mind that in the end, the choice you make, makes you."

And, of course, the choices made by the leader count most of all because they ultimately make, or break, your team.

Mental, moral, and physical Condition—in balance—are crucial to effective leadership. A leader who lacks physical Condition is less likely to summon the mental strength to stand up and fight for beliefs and convictions. You may have observed how those who weaken themselves physically often fall prey to an assortment of lapses in the area of good judgment.

Condition—physical, mental, and moral—is essential to being an effective and consistent leader. That's why Condition is in the center of the pyramid, so close to the heart of the structure.

COACH WOODEN'S X'S AND O'S:

CONDITION

- Character constitutes a component of Condition.

- What you do off the job is directly related to how well you do on the job.

- Moderation and balance are significant factors in attaining proper Condition.

- Physical Condition is impossible without mental and moral Condition.

Skill

WHEN YOU ARE THROUGH LEARNING,

YOU ARE THROUGH.

What a leader learns after having learned it all counts most of all.

Fundamentals in basketball means having comprehensive knowledge of the X's and O's and physical mechanics of the game—where to go and when to go there; how to shoot a shot or block a shot correctly.

We can appreciate that Skill is a requirement not only in basketball for both a coach and the players, but for any leader and organization. You must know what you're doing. Thus, Skill is at the very heart of the pyramid.

Know your job and be able to do it quickly and correctly. Knowledge of and the ability to execute your responsibilities will separate you from most of the competition. This means being prepared to do all that your job requires.

Mr. Wooden saw many coaches who could teach offense but were limited in their knowledge of defense. As a coach, he had players who were skilled shooters, but couldn't get open. Others were skilled at getting open, but couldn't shoot.

> *Push yourself to keep learning or you will stay as close to the bottom as to the top.*

Whether in basketball or in business, you must be able to "get open" and "shoot." One without the other makes you a partial performer: one who can be replaced because your skills are incomplete; one whose leadership falls short because of your own limitations when it comes to knowing your job.

The skills necessary for leadership differ from organization to organization. Those required to manage a restaurant differ from those of a sales manager, just as coaching basketball has different requirements from coaching baseball.

But regardless of the skills a particular profession requires, you must master them.

You must also be fully aware that mastery is a lifelong process of learning. The best leaders are those who realize it's what you learn after you know it all that counts most.

COACH WOODEN'S X'S AND O'S:

SKILL

- Complete competence is required. You must be able to execute all elements of your job or you are a partial performer.

- Experience is valuable. Skill is more valuable. Together they are invaluable.

- Skill means you can execute all facets of your job properly and quickly.

- Knowing what you're supposed to do means little if you don't have the Skill to do it.

Team Spirit

THE STAR OF YOUR TEAM IS THE TEAM.

"We" supersedes "me."

Initially, Mr. Wooden defined Team Spirit as "a willingness to lose oneself in the group for the good of the group."

Something about this definition was bothersome to him, but he couldn't put his finger on the problem.

Then one morning at breakfast he read a magazine article about a person who was described as having "an eagerness" to do some professional activity he was involved in. Coach Wooden recognized what had been wrong in his initial definition of Team Spirit.

A "willingness" to be selfless does not satisfy his requirements. It suggests begrudgingly doing what is required for the team's welfare. Coach Wooden wanted each player to be eager to sacrifice personal interests for the good of the group. Thus, as the pyramid was nearing its final form, he changed that one word in the definition: "willingness" became "eagerness."

> *Unselfish team play and team spirit are two of the foremost essentials for our success.*

Team Spirit—an eagerness to sacrifice personal interests or glory for the welfare of the group—is a tangible living force that transforms individuals who are "doing their jobs willingly" into an organization whose members are dedicated and eager to work at their highest level for the good of the group.

When this happens, the result is transformative. Just as Enthusiasm ignites Industriousness, Team Spirit is a catalyst for raising all the supporting qualities of the Pyramid to extraordinary heights because it creates a deep desire to do everything within your potential to strengthen your team.

When Team Spirit exists within your organization, the resulting productivity is exponential: your team becomes greater than the sum of its players; the organization greater than the talent and size of its personnel.

CEOs increasingly are media personalities whose own star—they seem to believe—shines brighter than the organization they lead.

There is only one star of importance: the team. The player or leader who seeks to have his or her star shine brighter than the group's is someone Mr. Wooden would want to neither coach nor play for.

COACH WOODEN'S X'S AND O'S:

TEAM SPIRIT

- Comprehend the difference between "willingness" and "eagerness," "selfishness" and "selflessness." Teach your team the difference.

- Team Spirit means you are willing to sacrifice personal considerations for the welfare of the organization.

- Team Spirit starts at the top. The leader, you, must personify Team Spirit.

- There is only one star that matters. The team is the star that matters.

GETTING TO THE TOP:
TRADEMARKS OF GREATNESS

The Good Book says, "As ye sow, so shall ye reap." The three tiers of the Pyramid that are now in place allow you to reap a rewarding and profound bounty, one that will produce two qualities closely identified with John Wooden and his teams. They are the two blocks near the apex of the Pyramid.

Poise

> IF YOU CAN MEET WITH TRIUMPH AND
> DISASTER AND TREAT THOSE TWO IMPOSTORS
> JUST THE SAME . . .
> —RUDYARD KIPLING

Just be yourself. Don't be rattled by events, whether good or bad. This may sound easy, but Poise can be a most elusive quality in challenging times. Leaders lacking Poise panic under pressure.

Poise means holding true to your belief that what counts most are your own high standards and making the effort to do the best of which you are capable regardless of how bad, or good, the situation may be.

Poise means being true to yourself even if it goes against popular sentiment, even if you must stand alone. It means avoiding pose or pretense, comparing yourself to others, acting like someone you're not. It means having a brave heart in all circumstances.

You'll know you possess Poise when you achieve what Rudyard Kipling described above in his poem written a hundred years ago.

That's Poise—not being thrown off stride in what you believe or how you behave because of outside events— "keeping your head when all about you are losing theirs."

The competitive environment challenges your composure and equanimity on a continuing basis as the stakes get high. Few characteristics are more valuable to a leader than Poise—especially under pressure. And pressure is what leaders are paid to deal with.

When Poise is present, you'll perform at your own personal best because Poise precludes panic. You'll understand what you're supposed to do, and do it even when the odds are against you, even when the experts say you'll fail.

How do you acquire Poise? In fact, you don't. Poise acquires you. It is part of the harvest you reap near the top of the Pyramid. Suddenly it is there, part of you and your leadership style and substance: Poise. It also becomes the style and substance of your organization.

Have respect for, without fear of,
every opponent, and confidence without
cockiness in regard to yourself.

COACH WOODEN'S X'S AND O'S:

POISE

- Poise means being true to oneself—not getting rattled, thrown off balance regardless of circumstances.

- You don't acquire Poise; it acquires you after you've prepared properly. The first 12 blocks of the Pyramid—personal qualities—are Coach Wooden's road map to proper preparation.

- Poise means avoiding pose or pretense, comparing yourself to others, or acting like something you're not.

- Poise means staying cool, calm, and collected when things really heat up.

Confidence

> YOU MUST EARN THE RIGHT TO BE CONFIDENT,
> THE KIND OF CONFIDENCE THAT COMES FROM
> PROPER PREPARATION.

The strongest steel is well-founded self-belief. It is earned, not given. Self-belief is the knowledge that your preparation is complete, that you have done all things possible to ready yourself and your organization for the competition in whatever form it arrives.

Confidence cannot be grafted on artificially. Real abiding Confidence, like Poise, is earned only by tenaciously attaining those assets that allow you to reach your own level of competency. For John Wooden, those assets are contained in and offered by the aforementioned personal characteristics and qualities of the Pyramid of Success.

Confidence must be monitored so that it does not spoil—rot—and become arrogance, the feeling of superiority that fosters an assumption that past success can be repeated automatically without the same hard effort that brought it about in the first place.

Thus, Coach Wooden has never gone into a game assuming victory. Neither did he ever assume defeat. He assumed nothing other than that he had taught those under his supervision how to bring out their best in competition. "Every opponent is to be respected; no opponent is to be feared if you have prepared properly." This is what he taught those under his supervision.

In fact, the quality, or lack thereof, of the competition had nothing to do with his level of Confidence. Rather, he drew strength from the sure knowledge that he had done all things possible to prepare himself and the team to perform at their highest level.

The competition may perform at a higher level, or not. He didn't concern himself with the competition's potential. His focus was on achieving his own potential as a leader and teaching his players how to do it as a team, an organiza-tion exhibiting the crowning characteristic of his pyramid.

Success requires Poise and Confidence, which come with proper preparation. It is the belief of John Wooden that acquiring the personal characteristics and values of the pyramid is, in fact, maximum preparation.

When you have prepared properly—and do not under-estimate the great challenge of proper and complete preparation—you will acquire the final—ultimate—block of the Pyramid of Success.

You must earn the right
to be confident.

COACH WOODEN'S X'S AND O'S:

CONFIDENCE

- Believe in yourself and others will believe in you.

- Well-founded Confidence is contagious.

- Confidence must not become arrogance.

- All supporting tiers of the Pyramid of Success give you the right to be Confident (and have Poise).

Beyond the winning and the goal,
beyond the glory and the fame,
He feels the flame within his soul,
born of the spirit of the game.
And where the barriers may wait,
built up by the opposing Gods,
He finds a thrill in bucking fate
and riding down the endless odds.

Where others wither in the fire
or fall below some raw mishap.
Where others lag behind or tire
and break beneath the handicap,
He finds a new and deeper thrill
to take him on the uphill spin,
Because the test is greater still,
and something he can revel in.
[Emphasis mine—SJ.]

—GRANTLAND RICE FROM
"THE GREAT COMPETITOR"

WHAT IT'S ALL ABOUT

Competitive Greatness

A GOAL BEYOND VICTORY,

A STANDARD ABOVE WINNING.

For over half a century, John Wooden has defined Competitive Greatness as follows: *Performing at your best when your best is needed; a real love for the hard battle.*

The great competitors he has played for, coached, and admired through many decades share a joy derived from the struggle itself—the journey—because only in that great effort of preparation and performance is there opportunity to bring forth your best, a personal greatness that cannot be diminished or dismissed because of a final score or the bottom line.

Competitive Greatness, for John Wooden, is not defined by Rudyard Kipling's "triumph" nor denied by "disaster." It exists in what precedes those two "impostors" and their accomplices fame, fortune, and power—conventional measurements of Competitive Greatness (and success) that Mr. Wooden reconfigured long ago. Competitive Greatness exists in the journey and culminates in the tough competitive fight in which you and your organization are at your best because you've prepared to the full extent of your abilities.

Subsequently, there is nothing tiresome for Mr. Wooden in the old adage, "When the going gets tough, the tough get going." He has tried hard to meet that criterion and teach it to others throughout his career.

This is one of the most crucial concepts a leader can carry and convey to those within the organization: namely, a love for the hard battle and the test it provides against a worthy opponent. The struggle is to be welcomed, never feared.

When you define success as John Wooden does, the only thing to fear is your own unwillingness to make the effort— 100 percent—to achieve your potential in leadership and teach those on your team how to achieve Competitive Greatness as an organization.

A Great Competitor welcomes the worthy opponent and the hard battle and defines success, first and foremost, by performing at their best when their very best is needed. A great leader teaches the organization to do the same. He also teaches that the "score" will then take care of itself.

When this occurs, it means you have arrived at the top, prepared to bring out the best in yourself and those under your leadership. You are a Great Competitor who leads a team capable of Competitive Greatness.

The struggle itself—the journey—is what gives value to the prize and is something the great competitive leader truly revels in. It is your responsibility to teach those under your supervision the same.

COACH WOODEN'S X'S AND O'S:

COMPETITIVE GREATNESS

- Competitive Greatness is brought forth only in the hard battle with a worthy opponent.

- Competitive Greatness is not defined by victory or denied by defeat, but by being your best when your best is required.

- Teach your team to welcome setbacks, stiff opposition, and contrary conditions. It offers the opportunity to separate themselves from all the others.

- Preparation—the first four tiers of the Pyramid of Success—is the prelude to being at your best when your best is needed: Competitive Greatness.

SUMMARY

- A pyramid has traditionally symbolized longevity and durability, strength and power.

- John Wooden chose the pyramid structure because it offered a format that was an effective teaching tool: each block assigned a value, each tier built on what came before. All leading to the apex—Success: peace of mind that is a direct result of self-satisfaction in knowing you made the effort to become the best you are capable of becoming.

- "Work" for most means going through the motions. Mr. Wooden had something else in mind and chose a word to reflect that: Industriousness.

- Industriousness is not possible unless it is partnered with Enthusiasm. Together they become the engine that drives everything forward with great power.

- Most everything that we do involves working with others. Mr. Wooden chose three blocks that are necessary for this to be done well: Friendship, Loyalty, and Cooperation. Together they represent the "working together" blocks in the Pyramid's foundation.

- Self-Control, Alertness, Initiative, and Intentness extend the foundation's characteristics and provide support for the heart of the pyramid.

- The heart of the Pyramid of Success is Condition (physical, mental, and moral), Skill, and Team Spirit.

- Near the apex, Coach Wooden placed Poise and Confidence. They come to you with proper preparation: the first three tiers.

- Competitive Greatness is possessing the ability to do your best when your best is needed. It comes with preparation and a love of the hard battle.

Personal greatness is not determined by the size of the job, but by the size of the effort that one puts into the job. This applies to everyone on your team.

FAITH AND PATIENCE: SYMBOLIC MORTAR

John Wooden added "mortar" at the top of the pyramid with the qualities of Patience and Faith.

They are symbolic and remind us that Patience and Faith must be present throughout the pyramid, holding the blocks and tiers firmly in place. A leader must have Faith that things will work out as they should—a boundless belief in the future.

A wise leader also knows that good things take time. If difficult goals could be achieved quickly, more people would be achievers. But most people—many leaders—lack Patience.

Success is always attainable when defined correctly; that is, making the effort—100 percent—to do the best of which you are capable. The 15 personal qualities of the pyramid are Coach Wooden's building blocks for success. You, and no one else, control whether you achieve success. You have it within your grasp, within your own power, to make the total effort. As leader, you have the responsibility to teach your organization how to do it.

Ultimately, the words of Joshua Hugh Wooden, Coach's father, describe it well: "When you've done your best, you may call yourself a success." You may also call yourself a Great Competitor—a leader who resides at the top of the pyramid where success and you are one and the same.

Big things are accomplished only through
the perfection of minor details.

SUCCESS

As a teacher, coach, and leader, John Wooden's goal has always been to help members of the team achieve their potential both individually and as a group.

The 15 personal qualities of the Pyramid are a simple way of illustrating what he required. In clear terms, it shows what he expected of them and what they could expect from him. As a teacher, success was his subject, the Pyramid of Success was his textbook.

Success may result in winning, but
winning does not necessarily
make you a success. Success, as I
define it, is harder to achieve.

SUMMARY

For John Wooden, success comes from the knowledge that you made the full effort to do the best of which you are capable.

When asked, "Coach Wooden, how did you win those championships?" he answers as follows: "I didn't win a single championship. Our team did. I like to believe that my teaching helped them accomplish that. The quality of my teaching and leadership and the effort I put into it is where I found—and continue to find—my defining and ultimate success. Not in the final score." But he will usually add, "And if the final score was to my liking, that made it all the better."

While others will judge you strictly in relation to somebody or something else—the final score, the bottom line—this is neither the most demanding nor the most productive standard. Throughout John Wooden's career, he did not allow others to define success for him, to impose their version of success on his leadership.

He sums it up simply: "If I did my best I believed in my heart that I was a success. Whether our team won a championship or not had little to do with my final reckoning of my success."

COMPASS CHECK

✴ SUCCESS IN LEADERSHIP ✴

• What is your personal definition of Success?

_____

_____

_____

_____

_____

_____

_____

_____

_____

_____

_____

_____

- What is your evaluation of John Wooden's definition of Success—its relevance, applicability, and effectiveness?

_____

_____

_____

_____

_____

_____

_____

✳ **CREATING YOUR OWN PYRAMID** ✳

The Foundation

INDUSTRIOUSNESS

- Select one individual in your past experience, personal or otherwise (i.e., historical figure, personal contact, book or movie character, etc.), who best personifies Industriousness. Describe in what way this person exemplifies it.

_____

_____

_____

_____

_____

_____

- Excluding yourself, who best exhibits Industriousness on your team? Describe the manner in which this person displays it.

_____

_____

_____

_____

_____

_____

_____

_____

_____

- How can you encourage Industriousness beyond whatever you currently do?

_____

_____

_____

_____

_____

_____

_____

_____

_____

ENTHUSIASM

- Select one individual in your past experience, personal or otherwise (i.e., historical figure, personal contact, book or movie character, etc.), who best personifies Enthusiasm. Describe in what way this person exemplifies it.

_____

_____

_____

_____

_____

_____

_____

- Excluding yourself, who best exhibits Enthusiasm on your team? Describe the manner in which this person displays it.

_____

_____

_____

_____

_____

_____

_____

- How can you encourage Enthusiasm beyond whatever you currently do?

_____

_____

_____

_____

_____

_____

_____

FRIENDSHIP

- Select one individual in your past experience, personal or otherwise (i.e., historical figure, personal contact, book or movie character, etc.), who best personifies Friendship. Describe the way this person exemplifies it.

_____

_____

_____

_____

_____

_____

_____

_____

- Excluding yourself, who best exhibits Friendship on your team? Describe the manner in which this person displays it.

_____

_____

_____

_____

_____

_____

_____

_____

_____

- How can you encourage Friendship beyond whatever you currently do?

_____

_____

_____

_____

_____

_____

_____

_____

_____

LOYALTY

- Select one individual in your past experience, personal or otherwise (i.e., historical figure, personal contact, book or movie character, etc.), who best personifies Loyalty. Describe in what way this person exemplifies it.

_____

_____

_____

_____

_____

_____

_____

_____

- Excluding yourself, who best exhibits Loyalty on your team? Describe the manner in which this individual displays it.

_____

_____

_____

_____

_____

_____

_____

- How can you encourage Loyalty beyond whatever you currently do?

_____

_____

_____

_____

_____

_____

_____

_____

COOPERATION

- Select one individual in your past experience, personal or otherwise (i.e., historical figure, personal contact, book or movie character, etc.), who best personifies Cooperation. Describe in what way this person exemplifies it.

_____

_____

_____

_____

_____

_____

_____

- Excluding yourself, who best exhibits Cooperation on your team? Describe the manner in which this individual displays it.

_____

_____

_____

_____

_____

_____

_____

_____

_____

- How can you encourage Cooperation beyond whatever you currently do?

_____

_____

_____

_____

_____

_____

_____

_____

The Second Tier

SELF-CONTROL

- Select one individual in your past experience, personal or otherwise (i.e., historical figure, personal contact, book or movie character, etc.), who best personifies Self-Control. Describe in what way this person exemplifies it.

_____

_____

_____

_____

_____

_____

_____

- Excluding yourself, who best exhibits Self-Control on your team? Describe the manner in which this individual displays it.

_____

_____

_____

_____

_____

_____

_____

- How can you encourage Self-Control beyond whatever you currently do?

_____

_____

_____

_____

_____

_____

_____

ALERTNESS

- Select one individual in your past experience, personal or otherwise (i.e., historical figure, personal contact, book or movie character, etc.), who best personifies Alertness. Describe in what way this person exemplifies it.

_____

_____

_____

_____

_____

_____

_____

_____

- Excluding yourself, who best exhibits Alertness on your team? Describe the manner in which this person displays it.

_____

_____

_____

_____

_____

_____

_____

_____

- How can you encourage Alertness beyond whatever you currently do?

_____

_____

_____

_____

_____

_____

_____

_____

INITIATIVE

- Select one individual in your past experience, personal or otherwise (i.e., historical figure, personal contact, book or movie character, etc.), who best personifies Initiative. Describe in what way this individual exemplifies it.

_____

_____

_____

_____

_____

_____

_____

_____

- Excluding yourself, who best exhibits Initiative on your team? Describe the manner in which this person displays it.

_____

_____

_____

_____

_____

_____

_____

_____

- How can you encourage Initiative beyond whatever you currently do?

_____

_____

_____

_____

_____

_____

_____

INTENTNESS

- Select one individual in your past experience, personal or otherwise (i.e., historical figure, personal contact, book or movie character, etc.), who best personifies Intentness. Describe in what way this person exemplifies it.

_____

_____

_____

_____

_____

_____

_____

_____

- Excluding yourself, who best exhibits Intentness on your team? Describe the manner in which this individual displays it.

  _____

  _____

  _____

  _____

  _____

  _____

  _____

  _____

  _____

- How can you encourage Intentness beyond whatever you currently do?

  _____

  _____

  _____

  _____

  _____

  _____

  _____

  _____

  _____

The Third Tier

CONDITION

- Select one individual in your past experience, personal or otherwise (i.e., historical figure, personal contact, book or movie character, etc.), who best personifies Condition. Describe in what way this person exemplifies it.

_____

_____

_____

_____

_____

_____

_____

- Excluding yourself, who best exhibits Condition on your team? Describe the manner in which this person displays it.

_____

_____

_____

_____

_____

_____

_____

- How can you encourage Condition beyond whatever you currently do?

_____

_____

_____

_____

_____

_____

_____

SKILL

- Select one individual in your past experience, personal or otherwise (i.e., historical figure, personal contact, book or movie character, etc.), who best personifies Skill. Describe in what way this person exemplifies it.

_____

_____

_____

_____

_____

_____

_____

_____

_____

- Excluding yourself, who best exhibits Skill on your team? Describe the manner in which this individual displays it.

_____

_____

_____

_____

_____

_____

_____

_____

- How can you encourage Skill beyond whatever you currently do?

_____

_____

_____

_____

_____

_____

_____

_____

TEAM SPIRIT

- Select one individual in your past experience, personal or otherwise (i.e., historical figure, personal contact, book or movie character, etc.), who best personifies Team Spirit. Describe in what way this person exemplifies it.

_____

_____

_____

_____

_____

_____

_____

_____

- Excluding yourself, who best exhibits Team Spirit on your team? Describe the manner in which this individuals displays it.

_____

_____

_____

_____

_____

_____

_____

_____

- How can you encourage Team Spirit beyond whatever you currently do?

_____

_____

_____

_____

_____

_____

The Fourth Tier

POISE

- Select one individual in your past experience, personal or otherwise (i.e., historical figure, personal contact, book or movie character, etc.), who best personifies Poise. Describe in what way this person exemplifies it.

_____

_____

_____

_____

_____

_____

_____

_____

- Excluding yourself, who best exhibits Poise on your team? Describe the manner in which this individual displays it.

_____

_____

_____

_____

_____

_____

_____

_____

_____

- How can you encourage Poise beyond whatever you currently do?

_____

_____

_____

_____

_____

_____

_____

_____

_____

CONFIDENCE

- Select one individual in your past experience, personal or otherwise (i.e., historical figure, personal contact, book or movie character, etc.), who best personifies Confidence. Describe in what way this person exemplifies it.

_____

_____

_____

_____

_____

_____

_____

_____

- Excluding yourself, who best exhibits Confidence on your team? Describe the manner in which this individual displays it.

_____

_____

_____

_____

_____

_____

_____

- How can you encourage Confidence beyond whatever you currently do?

_____

_____

_____

_____

_____

_____

_____

The Pinnacle

COMPETITIVE GREATNESS

- Select one individual in your past experience, personal or otherwise (i.e., historical figure, personal contact, book or movie character, etc.), who best personifies Competitive Greatness. Describe in what way this person exemplifies it.

_____

_____

_____

_____

_____

_____

_____

_____

- Excluding yourself, who best exhibits Competitive Greatness on your team? Describe the manner in which this individual displays it.

_____

_____

_____

_____

_____

_____

_____

_____

- How can you encourage Competitive Greatness beyond whatever you currently do?

_____

_____

_____

_____

_____

_____

_____

_____

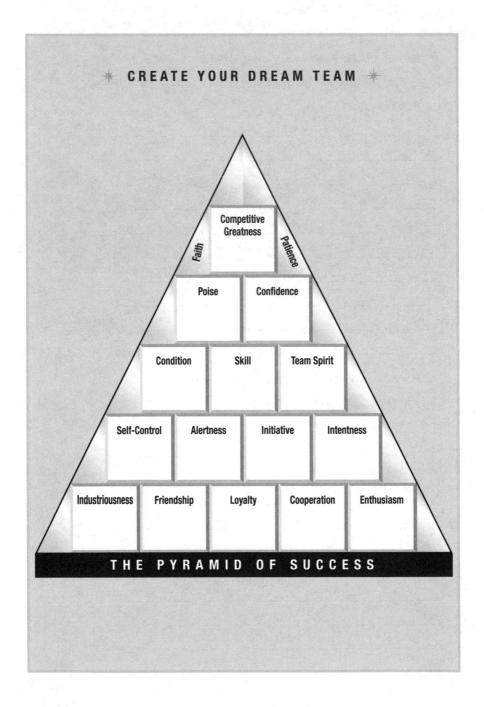

✳ **CREATE YOUR DREAM TEAM** ✳

THE PYRAMID OF SUCCESS

- In the Pyramid on the facing page, write the name of the individual who best personifies the personal quality of each block.

_____

_____

_____

_____

_____

_____

_____

_____

_____

_____

_____

_____

_____

_____

_____

_____

_____

_____

• Evaluate how you can incorporate elements of each Dream Team individual you selected into your own skills as leader.

_____

PART III

12 LESSONS IN LEADERSHIP

LEADERSHIP LESSON #1: GOOD VALUES ATTRACT GOOD PEOPLE

Treat all people with dignity and respect.

What I Learned

BY KAREEM ABDUL-JABBAR
UCLA VARSITY, 1967–69;
THREE NCAA NATIONAL CHAMPIONSHIPS

John Wooden built his basketball program a certain way—athletically, ethically, morally—because he believed it would attract a certain type of person, the kind of individual he wanted on the team. He was right.

I chose UCLA and Coach Wooden in large part because of those values. It was like that movie, *Field of Dreams*: "Build it and they will come." He built it. We came.

What It Means

BY STEVE JAMISON

Kareem Abdul-Jabbar is "the most valuable player to a team in the history of the college game," in the judgment of Coach John Wooden. Abdul-Jabbar went on to become the NBA's all-time scoring leader.

As a high school player at New York's Power Memorial Academy, Abdul-Jabbar was the most sought-after student-athlete in America. The coaching community was in general agreement: the school he chose would soon be the national champion.

Why did this extremely talented young man, a native New Yorker who wanted to stay close to home, choose to attend a university that was on the other side of the country—UCLA? The simple answer? Values.

Kareem Abdul-Jabbar had become aware of the values and standards of UCLA, including full integration and high academic standards. He had also become aware of the character of its coach, John Wooden. Former players had repeatedly told the young high school star, "Coach Wooden is color blind when it comes to race."

UCLA and its varsity basketball coach were the beneficiaries of the great athletic and academic talent of Kareem Abdul-Jabbar because he was drawn to their shared values and standards. He was not the only individual to choose UCLA over other opportunities because of its outstanding reputation.

Character—doing the right thing—is fundamental to successful leadership.

Values, standards, and character mattered to Abdul-Jabbar and his parents, Cora and Lewis Sr. They also mattered to John Wooden. And in large part he learned them from his dad, Joshua Hugh Wooden, and his three influential mentors, Earl Warriner, Glenn Curtis, and Ward "Piggy" Lambert.

You and your organization's good values, standards, and productive attitudes will attract individuals who have the same.

My Perspective | by John Wooden

Aristotle said, "We are what we repeatedly do." He was referring to character—the habits of our daily behavior that reveal who and what we are. I wanted to create good habits in those under my leadership. Standards, values, and attitudes were important to me. I wanted them to matter to those I taught.

Here's a good definition of character: respect for your-self, respect for others, respect for the rules. For those I coached, I believed that character started with little things like picking up after yourself (rather than expecting the team manager to clean up your mess) and extends to big things like honesty, compassion, and the 15 personal quali-ties I placed in the Pyramid of Success. I sought individuals who had character rather than individuals who were just characters.

Leadership is about more than making people do what you say. A prison guard can do that. A good leader creates belief—in the leader, in the organization, in its mission. This is difficult to do where a vacuum of values exists, where the only thing that matters is a bottom line, winning the race. All kinds of bad things can happen when the only thing that matters is "winning." Just read the newspapers today and you'll find all the evidence you need that this is true.

The kind of people I wanted to have running the race with me were those with whom I shared a code of behav-ior—values and standards. This didn't always happen—after all, people are human—but one of the primary ways to en-sure that this occurs is to make your values visible, to let the outside world know what you stand for and who you are.

In doing so, you will attract those who share your prin-ciples and standards.

Your behavior as leader—what you do—creates the en-vironment in which the team functions.

COACH WOODEN'S X'S AND O'S:

GOOD VALUES ATTRACT GOOD PEOPLE

- Good values are like a magnet. So are bad values.

- Make your values visible; what you do is who you are. Who you are is what the organization becomes. People actually do "follow the leader."

- Character starts with little things and extends to big things. Ralph Waldo Emerson says, "Character is cumulative."

- Select people who are seeking you and your organization. Perhaps they recognize shared values, standards, and attitudes.

LEADERSHIP LESSON #2: USE THE MOST POWERFUL FOUR-LETTER WORD

What I Learned

BY JIM POWERS
SOUTH BEND CENTRAL HIGH, 1941–43;
INDIANA STATE TEACHERS COLLEGE, 1947–48

During World War II I'd been shot down in a B-24 bombing raid on Italian oil fields and almost got killed. I had a fear of flying after that—would not get on a plane.

When I got out of the military, I went to Indiana State, where John Wooden was head coach. He had been my coach at South Bend Central High School. One week we were scheduled to play a game in New York, which meant an airplane trip to the East Coast. There was no way I intended to get on that plane. Absolutely no way.

When Coach Wooden found out about my problem and why I wouldn't fly, he said the solution was simple: "Nobody on this team gets left behind." So he rounded up cars, and we drove to New York.

If you played for John Wooden, you were part of his family. We felt like we were in a family. And we were. In fact, I still feel like I'm part of his family.

Be more concerned with what you can do
for others than what others can do for you.
You'll be surprised at the result.

What It Means

BY STEVE JAMISON

John Wooden did not consider those he coached as plug-in parts, "jocks" whose value was in direct proportion to the number of points they could score. In a very real sense, he felt each student-athlete was a member of his extended family. And he reminds us, "Love is present in a good family." You must demonstrate it in appropriate ways with support and concern within a disciplined environment.

In the early days of his teaching, Coach Wooden started each season by trying to express his intention to be impartial with the following statement: "I will like you all the same." And then he would add, "And, I will treat you all the same." Of course, this turned out to be false.

> The smallest good deed is better than the best intention.

There were some players on the squad that Coach Wooden could hardly stand, and it troubled him because he felt strongly that a leader should be "friends" with those under his supervision. Furthermore, he recognized that he did not treat a hardworking player the same as one who was less so. Treating everyone the same, he soon realized, was unfair.

During this period he read a statement by Amos Alonzo Stagg, Chicago's legendary football coach, that helped him reformulate his perspective on the relationship between a leader and the team. Coach Stagg said, "I loved all my players the same; I just didn't like them all the same."

By the time Coach Wooden arrived at UCLA, his message to the players at the beginning of each season was as follows: "I will not like you all the same, but I will love you all the same. Furthermore, I will try very hard not to let my feelings interfere with my judgment of your performance. You receive the treatment you earn and deserve."

My Perspective | by John Wooden

Nobody cares how much you know until they know how much you care. The individuals on our UCLA teams became true members of my extended family.

I once bailed a player out of jail for a driving violation even though it went against conference rules. These and other acts of kindness and concern were small gestures, but a direct result of the feelings—the love—I had for those under my supervision. It's vital to let those you lead know you care. First, of course, you must have that care in your heart for those you lead.

And while I could have great love in my heart for those under my supervision, I would not tolerate behavior from anyone that was detrimental, or potentially detrimental, to the welfare of our group.

For me, it is possible to have the greatest care and concern for someone and bench, suspend, or even remove him from the team.

COACH WOODEN'S X'S AND O'S:

USE THE MOST POWERFUL FOUR-LETTER WORD

- The people in your organization are your extended family.

- Coach Stagg's advice is apt: "Love" is more important than "like."

- Treating everyone "the same" is not fair. Each member of your team should get what they earn and deserve.

- Seek opportunities to show you care. The smallest gestures often make the biggest difference.

- Love does not mean you tolerate bad behavior.

LEADERSHIP LESSON #3:
CALL YOURSELF A TEACHER

What I Learned

BY DENNY CRUM
UCLA VARSITY, 1958–59; ASSISTANT COACH, 1969–71;
TWO NCAA NATIONAL CHAMPIONSHIPS;
HEAD COACH, UNIVERSITY OF LOUISVILLE

Coach Wooden's philosophy was to teach what was necessary to make UCLA a better team—the best we could be. Teach it; practice it. The details and all of the fundamentals were his main concern. Thus, he never talked about the winning or the losing. He wouldn't come in before a game and say, "This team is tied with us in the conference, so we've got to step it up tonight. Let's win this one."

He just wasn't concerned about the opponents and what they might be up to—didn't even scout most of them. He felt that if he taught us what was necessary, we'd do fine. He was really a good teacher.

Each member of your team has the
potential for personal greatness;
a leader's job is to teach them how to do it.

What It Means

BY STEVE JAMISON

The outside world knows your profession—what you do—by the title on your business card: sales manager, CEO, production supervisor, or something else. However, don't be misled by what it says on your card.

In the eyes of many observers, John Wooden's business card should say "Coach," but this is not what he would choose. From the earliest years he has called himself a teacher.

The most effective leaders are good teachers. What does an effective leader teach? Regardless of context, it is the same, namely, how to perform at your highest level in ways that serve the welfare of the organization.

If there is a single reason the UCLA Bruins enjoyed success in basketball while John Wooden was head coach, it was because he learned how to be a good teacher, not only of the X's and O's, but of the more elusive qualities such as Team Spirit, Cooperation, Initiative, and the other components of his Pyramid of Success.

As a young and inexperienced coach, John Wooden was impatient. When things weren't done correctly "right now," he pushed harder and talked louder.

Increasingly he began using the Four Laws of Learning: Explanation, Demonstration, Imitation—correction when necessary—and Repetition. These are the same as the Four

Laws of Teaching, and both require great patience. This is why he included Patience in the pyramid.

An effective teacher must also have a good hat rack, one with plenty of hooks for all the different "hats" you wear: teacher, of course, but also disciplinarian, counselor, role model, psychologist, motivator, timekeeper, quality control expert, talent judge, referee, organizer, and more.

> *An effective leader is very good at listening.*
> *It's difficult to listen when you are talking.*

My Perspective | by John Wooden

A good teacher is a good student, a lifelong learner. No two people are the same. Each individual under your leadership is unique. There is no formula that applies to all when it comes to teaching and leading. All won't follow; some need a push. Some you drive, others you lead. Recognizing the difference requires a knowledge of human nature. That's where being a good student helps you in your leadership.

I taught by offering information in small bite-size pieces rather than large chunks that couldn't be assimilated easily. I tried to set the example I wanted those I coached to follow. The greatest teaching tool is your own example. I studied human nature. I kept learning. I kept teaching.

And when I asked the question 100 times, I asked it again: "How can I help our team improve?"

COACH WOODEN'S X'S AND O'S:

CALL YOURSELF A TEACHER

- The greatest teaching tool is your own example. Your deeds count more than your words.

- Be patient. People progress at different speeds.

- A good teacher wears many hats. Make sure they all fit your head.

- A good demonstration is more effective than a great description.

- A great leader is a teacher who is a lifelong student.

LEADERSHIP LESSON #4:
EMOTION IS YOUR ENEMY

What I Learned

BY FRED SLAUGHTER
UCLA VARSITY, 1962–64;
ONE NCAA NATIONAL CHAMPIONSHIP

There were four or five games in my career when we started out way behind like, 18–2—just getting killed. I'd look over

115

at Coach Wooden, and there he'd sit on the bench with his program rolled up in his hand—totally unaffected, almost like we were ahead. And I'd think to myself, "Hey, if he's not worried, why should I be worried?"

Instead of panic, I settled down, and so did the team. We won each of those games except one.

John Wooden was cool when it counted; his confidence and strength and attitude became our confidence, strength, and attitude. In three years on the UCLA varsity, I never once saw him get rattled, and we had some nerve-rattling games, including a last-second loss in the Final Four to Cincinnati.

Coach was cool, and he taught us to be the same. Especially under pressure.

What It Means

BY STEVE JAMISON

Extreme intensity—controlled and correctly directed—is an essential ingredient for unswerving—consistent—productivity and competitiveness. Emotionalism—temperamental flare-ups and drop-offs—makes consistent high performance impossible.

A leader controlled by emotions will produce a team whose trademark is the roller coaster—ups and downs in performance; unpredictability in effort and concentration; one day good, the next day bad. John Wooden has deep disdain for the "roller-coaster" pattern in both effort and performance.

Thus, he never gave rah-rah speeches or contrived pep talks. For every artificial emotional peak attained, you and your team will be subjected to a valley, a letdown.

> *If you let your emotions take over, you will be outplayed.*

Coach Wooden demanded intense and steady effort with the goal of producing consistent ongoing learning and improvement. This, in his view, was preferable to getting individuals heated up for some arbitrary peak in performance, which would be followed inevitably by a drop-off in effort and execution.

In all UCLA basketball practices and games, he demanded intensity that did not boil over into emotionalism and loss of self-control. Former UCLA center Bill Walton describes that intensity during a practice as equal to what he experienced in actual games—including games to decide a championship.

Ideally John Wooden wanted the team to improve during each practice and game—every day, each week—throughout the season until they were at their finest on the final day of the year.

Steady, constant, reliable, and complete effort that leads to improvement that was manifested in performance at an increasingly high standard was his goal. It is almost impossible to overstate the primacy of this goal in his leadership philosophy and methodology. To achieve it, Coach Wooden required emotional control both in himself and in those under his leadership. It took him many years before he mastered it, and even then not completely. He prized intensity and viewed emotionalism as a weakness.

> *Intensity makes you stronger. Emotionalism makes you weaker.*

My Perspective | by John Wooden

Some observers described me as being detached, almost stoic, on the bench during games. This could hardly be further from the truth, but it was a compliment nevertheless.

Emotionalism—ups and downs in moods, temperamental outbursts—is almost always counterproductive, at times ruinous.

I came to understand that if my own behavior was filled with outbursts, peaks and valleys of emotion and moods, I was sanctioning it for others. As the leader, my own behavior set the bounds of acceptability.

Subsequently, I became much more vigilant in controlling my feelings and behavior. My message to those I led was simple: "If you let your emotions take control, you have lost control. You are vulnerable." For those under my supervision to learn the lesson, however, I had to control my own behavior and emotions.

Subsequently, I never second-guessed myself for decisions and actions that didn't work out if they were made using my best judgment and all available information. It may have been a mistake, but it was not an error.

It becomes an error, however, when the choice was made because emotions spilled over and diminished the quality of my decision making. Early in my career the errors were common; there were fewer as my emotional control became more disciplined.

A leader defined by intensity is a stronger leader. A leader ruled by emotions is weak, the team vulnerable.

COACH WOODEN'S X'S AND O'S:

EMOTION IS YOUR ENEMY

- Seek and prize consistently applied high intensity.

- Emotionalism makes a leader (and team) vulnerable.

- Emotional peaks lead to emotional valleys.

- Consistency in high performance is the mark of a champion.

LEADERSHIP LESSON #5: IT TAKES 10 HANDS TO SCORE A BASKET

What I Learned

BY RAY REGAN
SOUTH BEND CENTRAL HIGH SCHOOL VARSITY, 1938–39

I remember we used to have a showboat on our team, a player who was always yelling for the ball, and then once he got it would keep it until he took a shot. Then he'd start yelling for the ball again. He was having trouble with Coach Wooden's concept of teamwork and sharing.

One day Coach decided to teach this guy a lesson. He took us aside and said to pass the basketball to the showboat and then immediately run to the middle of the court—

all four of his teammates—sit down, and let him face the other squad alone.

It was Coach's way of showing that everybody helps everybody or nothing gets done. The showboat started passing the ball after that.

> *Be sure you acknowledge and give credit to*
> *a teammate who hits you with a scoring pass*
> *or for any fine play he may make.*

What It Means

by Steve Jamison

In basketball, a field goal is scored only after several hands have touched the ball. In business, the "ball" is knowledge, experience, ideas, and information. Whether on the court

or off, that "ball" must be shared quickly and efficiently to achieve success.

A salesperson, or any other member of your organization who has the "ball," must share it. A "me first" person puts the team second. That person is not a team player.

Getting those under your supervision to think "team first" starts when you teach every person in the organization that their role is important in some way to the welfare of the group.

All roles, every job, contribute in their own way to the success of the organization. Some individuals are more difficult to replace than others because of differences in ability, but every person you bring into your organization contributes—or should— to the overall success of the group.

> *Have one team, not starters and substitutes. No one feels good being a "substitute."*

Each must feel valued, from the secretary to the salesperson to the senior manager. When they understand that they are contributing members of the team and that their role has value, good things will occur.

For this reason, Coach Wooden was the first in college basketball to insist on the "acknowledge your teammate" rule—namely, giving a nod or a wink to the player who gave an assist.

Coach Wooden wanted the player who scored a basket to understand that he was only as good as the team assisting him, that it takes 10 hands to score two points.

No matter how great your product, if one of your departments doesn't produce, you won't get the results you want. Everybody must do their job.

I told players that we, as a team, are like a powerful race car. Maybe a Bill Walton or Kareem Abdul-Jabbar is the big engine, but if one wheel is flat, we're going no place. And if we have brand new tires but the lug nuts are missing, the wheels come off. What good is the powerful engine then, when the wheels come off? Every part, big or small, on that race car matters. Everything contributes to the running of the race. And, of course, a car needs a driver. I was the driver.

I don't need scientific evidence to know that Rudyard Kipling was correct: "For the strength of the pack is the wolf; and the strength of the wolf is the pack."

That describes the relationship between the individual and the organization—the player and the team.

Acquire peace of mind by making the effort to become the best of which you are capable.

> ## COACH WOODEN'S X'S AND O'S:
>
> ### IT TAKES 10 HANDS TO SCORE A BASKET
>
> - The star of your team is the team. Both you and your organization must fully comprehend that fact.
>
> - The best talent doesn't always make the best team.
>
> - Teamwork means sharing—the ball, information, contacts, ideas.
>
> - An organization that lacks selflessness among its members is like a race car with a powerful engine and a flat tire. Everybody assists everybody.

LEADERSHIP LESSON #6:
LITTLE THINGS MAKE
BIG THINGS HAPPEN

What I Learned

BY LYNN SHACKLEFORD
UCLA VARSITY, 1967–69; THREE NCAA NATIONAL
CHAMPIONSHIPS

There was logic to every move. Details of socks, shoelaces, and hair length led to details of running plays, handling the ball, and scoring points—hundreds of small things done exactly as Coach Wooden wanted them done.

Everything was related to everything else; nothing was left to chance. Sloppiness was not allowed in anything, not in passing, shooting, or trimming your fingernails and tucking in your jersey.

Coach Wooden taught that great things can only be accomplished by doing the little things right. Doing things right became a habit with us. Habits stand up under pressure.

Big things are accomplished
only through the perfection
of minor details.

What It Means

BY STEVE JAMISON

Leadership often places such emphasis on reaching a distant and lofty goal (annual sales results in business; winning a championship in sports) that inadequate attention is paid to what it takes to get there—the day-by-day, minute-to-minute relevant details of how you do your job.

Sloppiness in tending to details is common—the norm—in sports and in most organizations. When it occurs, blame rests with you, the leader, not with those in the organization.

High performance is achieved only through the identification and perfection of the small but relevant details, little things done well.

Minor details, like pennies, add up. A good banker isn't careless with pennies; a good leader isn't careless with details.

Those under your leadership must be taught that little things make big things happen. First they must be taught that there are no big things, only a logical accumulation of little things done at a high standard of execution.

At UCLA John Wooden worked hard to ensure that standards—the norm—in the area of details were set extremely high. "Normal" was abnormally high.

Outside observers and even some players thought the hundreds of specifics he selected for attention and perfection were foolish. Coach Wooden knew that those details—for example, putting on sweat socks correctly—were the foundation of future success and competitive greatness. Your ability to see this profound connection in your own work is essential to good leadership.

While Coach Wooden strove for perfection, "perfectionist" is not a description he would choose for himself. Perfection, he believes, is not attainable by mortal man. Striving for it with utmost effort, however, is attainable. Thus, he was relentless in looking for ways to improve performance. When he identified something that could move a team closer to perfection, he taught them how to do it.

No relevant detail is too small to be done correctly.

My Perspective | by John Wooden

consider each detail like a rivet in the wing of an airplane. Remove one rivet from the wing and it makes no difference. Remove enough of them, however, and the wing falls off.

I didn't want anything to fall off when it came to the performance of the UCLA Bruins basketball team in practice or in games. Thus, every detail that was relevant was important and deserved to be done the right way.

Just as there is a correct way to put on sweat socks, there is a correct way of executing everything in basketball. There is a correct way of doing every job in every organization.

For me, there isn't an "approximate" way to shoot a jump shot. There is an exact and precise method for doing it, one that affords the best chance for making the shot with allowances for the specific situation. And this is true for all other aspects of playing the game.

My fervor to see that relevant details were perfected in all areas was intended to set the tone, in style and in substance, for how the UCLA Bruins conducted business. Our standards were very high in the execution of relevant details. Most observers saw only the trophy. Few comprehended the magnitude of perfected details preceding the trophy.

I love to see little things done correctly. In my experience, that may be as close to anything that I can identify as being "the secret of success": little things done right.

COACH WOODEN'S X'S AND O'S:

LITTLE THINGS MAKE BIG THINGS HAPPEN

- There are no big things; only an accumulation of little things that must be done well.

- Details are like rivets in the wing of an airplane. Remove enough of them and the wing falls off.

- Success starts from the ground up. Understand the relationship between "socks" and success.

- Talent must be nourished in an environment of high performance standards. Sloppiness breeds sloppiness. When it comes to details, teach good habits.

LEADERSHIP LESSON #7: MAKE EACH DAY YOUR MASTERPIECE

What I Learned

BY EDDIE POWELL
SOUTH BEND CENTRAL HIGH SCHOOL; PLAYER,
ASSISTANT COACH, INDIANA STATE TEACHERS COLLEGE,
1947–48; ASSISTANT COACH, UCLA, 1948–52

The South Bend Central team bus was scheduled to leave for our game against Mishawaka High School at exactly 6 p.m. All of us players were in our seats and ready to go except for two guys. They happened to be the co-captains of our team, the South Bend Central Bears. Probably our best players.

"Driver, what time do you have," Coach Wooden asked when he stepped on board the bus. The driver looked at his

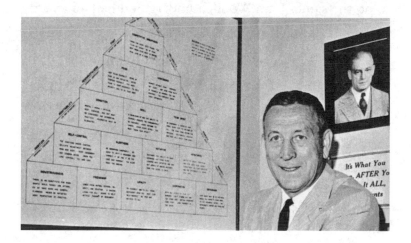

watch and said, "It's exactly 6 p.m., Coach." Coach Wooden replied, "Well, that's what time my watch says, too. I guess it must be 6 p.m." He looked hard at those two empty seats and said to the driver, "Let's go." Coach left our two most valuable players behind. Nobody was late after that. The lesson was passed on from team to team each year. Time meant a lot to Coach Wooden.

Activity to produce real results must be organized and executed meticulously. Otherwise, it's no different from children running around the playground at recess.

What It Means

BY STEVE JAMISON

There is not enough time. A leader must be very astute in using time productively and teaching those in the organization to do the same. John Wooden understood he had exactly 210 hours of practice time to accomplish his teaching goals (105 practices, each two hours in length). Or, as journalists and fans would say, Coach Wooden had 210 hours to win a national championship—12,600 minutes of actual practice time during the regular season.

Coach Wooden placed great value on every single one of those 12,600 minutes; each was a never-to-be-regained opportunity to teach the team what they needed to know to achieve Competitive Greatness, to outscore the competition.

Time, used correctly, is perhaps your most important asset. Take it away and you have nothing. Wasting a single moment became painful for him, like throwing a gold coin into the ocean never to be recovered.

John Wooden's own appreciation for time may have begun with his father's advice in the Seven-Point Creed: "Make each day your masterpiece." It was Joshua Hugh Wooden's way of reminding his son to use time wisely, not wastefully. Time is invisible. Its effects are not.

> *If you do not have the time to do it right, when will you find the time to do it over?*

Only when you fully comprehend the significance of a single minute will you begin to treat the hour with respect. You will notice that successful leaders do not disrespect time.

Coach Wooden strove to make each meeting a masterpiece, each practice perfect. This came from his understanding that how you practice is how you play—in sports and elsewhere. He taught himself the mastery of using time to its greatest advantage.

My Perspective | by John Wooden

One of the very few rules I enforced from my first day of coaching until my last was as follows: "Be on time." Players—even assistant coaches—who broke this rule faced serious consequences.

Being late showed disrespect for time. I felt that one of the ways I could signal my own reverence for time was to insist on punctuality. And, to be punctual myself.

If a player appeared to be taking it easy during practice, not giving it everything he had, I told him sternly, "Don't think you can make up for it by working twice as hard tomorrow. If you have it within your power to work twice as hard, I want you to do it right now." This was another way of telling them not to waste time; to make this practice a masterpiece.

I believe effective organization of time—budgeting and managing time—was one of my assets as a coach. I understood how to use time to its most productive ends. Gradually, I had learned how to get the most out of a minute. In return, each minute gave back the most to our team.

I was never the greatest X's and O's coach around. Never. But I was among the best when it came to respecting and utilizing time. I valued it, gave it respect, and tried to make each minute a masterpiece.

> *It's what you learn*
> *after you know it all*
> *that counts.*

COACH WOODEN'S X'S AND O'S:

MAKE EACH DAY YOUR MASTERPIECE

- You have nothing without time. Treat it with great respect.

- A productive "quarter" begins with a masterful minute.

- Don't mistake activity for achievement.

- Treat time carelessly and it will do the same to you and your organization.

- Personal punctuality is a good way to teach respect for time.

LEADERSHIP LESSON #8:
THE CARROT IS
MIGHTIER THAN A STICK

What I Learned

BY BILL WALTON
UCLA VARSITY, 1972–74;
TWO NCAA NATIONAL CHAMPIONSHIPS

Coach Wooden expected you to be really good. Being really good was normal. He didn't think we needed to be complimented for doing what was normal.

However, as players, we knew we were rising to a greater level when we'd see that little smile on his face. When four

*Punishment invokes fear. I wanted a team whose
members were filled with pride, not fear.*

guys touched the ball in two seconds and the fifth guy hit a
lay-up, man, what a feeling!

I'd look over and see a nod, a little wink of approval
from my coach. I'm telling you a chill would run down my
spine. He was saying in his own way, "You just went beyond really good to being great." Then he would blow his
whistle and say, "Now do it again. Faster."

What It Means

BY STEVE JAMISON

A leader has a simple mission: to get those under his or her
supervision to work at their highest level of ability in ways

that best serve the team. Your skills as a leader who can motivate determine if and to what degree this occurs.

There are times when severe censure or penalty may be effective. Most often, however, a leader resorts to punishment because he lacks an understanding of its limitations as well as the skills necessary to create motivation based on pride, not fear.

John Wooden came to the conclusion that when choosing between the carrot and the stick as a motivational tool, the well-chosen carrot was almost always more powerful and long-lasting than the stick.

Common carrots in business include money, of course, advancement, awards, recognition, a corner office, a more prominent role on the team or in the organization. Carrots come in many forms.

Give me 100 percent. You can't make up for a poor effort today by giving 110 percent tomorrow. You don't have 110 percent. You only have 100 percent, and that's what I want from you right now.

However, Coach Wooden believes there is perhaps no stronger form of motivation—no better carrot—than approval from someone an individual truly respects, whose approval they seek.

He explains it like this: "I prefer to give a 'pat on the back' as a motivational tool, although sometimes the pat must be a little lower and a little harder."

Sincere approval instills pride. Punishment invokes fear. He wanted a team whose members were filled with pride rather than fear.

Pride in the team and its effort is a fundamental component of Competitive Greatness in the philosophy of John Wooden. Wise use of the carrot can facilitate this, especially in combination with prudent use of the stick.

The fear and ill feelings that arise from intimidation, punishment, and cruel words—common practices with dictator-style leaders—have less power than sincere praise.

It is very hard to influence in a positive and long-lasting way when you antagonize someone.

My Perspective | by John Wooden

Commendations and criticism exist, of course, within a framework of expectations—rules—regarding behavior from those in your organization.

When I was just starting out, I had lots of rules and very few suggestions. The rules were spelled out in black and white, and so were the penalties for breaking them.

When a player broke one of my rules, the punishment was automatic, enforced without discussion. And the punishment was often severe; in retrospect, often too severe.

Eventually I came to recognize that common sense is needed in deciding when and how penalties should be applied. Over the years I changed from having lots of rules and few suggestions to lots of suggestions and fewer rules.

To a large degree I replaced specific rules and penalties with strong suggestions and unspecified consequences. This gave me much greater discretion and allowed for more productive responses to misbehavior.

I came to believe as a coach and leader that if I conducted myself in a manner that earned the respect of those under my leadership, this same feeling would exist in them. When it did, I would gain one of the most powerful leadership tools available to a leader, namely, trust. Why? Because with respect comes trust by those on the team.

I tried hard to earn their respect and trust. Subsequently, when I gave my nod of approval, a wink, a pat on the back, it meant something. In fact, it meant a lot.

COACH WOODEN'S X'S AND O'S:

THE CARROT IS MIGHTIER THAN A STICK

- The most effective carrot is often a respected leader's praise. It creates pride.

- Don't give praise if you don't mean it. And even then don't give it too often.

- The purpose of criticism is to correct, improve, and change; rarely to humiliate or embarrass.

- It is difficult to effect positive change when you antagonize.

LEADERSHIP LESSON #9: MAKE GREATNESS AVAILABLE TO EVERYONE

What I Learned

BY DOUG MCINTOSH
UCLA VARSITY, 1964–66;
TWO NCAA NATIONAL CHAMPIONSHIPS

"You can always do more than you think you can." That's the biggest thing I got from Coach Wooden's teaching. There's always more inside if you're willing to work hard enough to bring it out.

Most of the time we don't recognize we have great potential inside. Coach brought out the potential in people. He taught mental readiness: "Be ready and your chance may come. If you are not ready, it may not come again."

Thus, he made me see there are no small opportunities. Every opportunity is big. If you only play for two minutes, make it the best two minutes possible.

> *Each member of your team has the potential for personal greatness; the leader's job is to help them achieve it.*

That's your opportunity, whether in basketball or in life. Be ready; make the most of it. It may not come again.

What It Means

BY STEVE JAMISON

John Wooden will not single out a "greatest UCLA player" or "greatest UCLA team." Who's #1? He will not say because it runs contrary to his concept of success; specifically, that personal greatness is measured against one's own potential, not that of someone else. Likewise, a team's greatness is measured against itself and no other.

He wanted the individuals under his supervision—players, assistant coaches, student managers, the trainer—to understand that the kind of greatness he sought and valued was available to each and every one of them: "Give me the best you've got. That's all I ask." Each member of the team

139

understood they could achieve greatness by doing what he asked. It was attainable by doing their job, fulfilling their role, at the highest level of their effort and ability. Success—Competitive Greatness—was available to everyone on every team ever coached by John Wooden.

Coach Wooden asked a player such as Bill Walton to strive to achieve his own potential—his own greatness—just as he wanted head manager Les Friedman to seek his own personal best in doing the job assigned.

> *"Make sure you can hold your head up high after the game." They all knew I wasn't talking about the final score.*

John Wooden recognized that Walton's contribution to the team could be more valuable than that of the eighth man on the bench or the head manager, but his true belief, deeply felt, was that each individual under his supervision could achieve personal greatness. Bill Walton might be more valuable and difficult to replace, but his potential for Competitive Greatness as measured by Coach Wooden was exactly the same for every individual on the team. This was a concept that he worked ceaselessly to instill in the minds of everyone he coached.

When leaders instill the belief that the opportunity for personal greatness exists within every job, every role, and each person on the team, they will find themselves in charge of extraordinary achievers and motivated and most productive organizations.

For this reason, Mr. Wooden has always been strongly against retiring a player's number because it, in effect, declares a particular individual as the greatest at that position. He feels this is dismissive of previous players who wore the number and achieved their own personal greatness.

My Perspective | by John Wooden

I stated the following very clearly in my teaching: "In whatever role I assign you, execute your responsibilities to the very best of your ability." Whether as a nonstarter or a star, I called on each to seek his own potential, his own greatness, not that of someone else.

For an organization to succeed, all members must achieve personal greatness; each in their own role that helps the team; each striving to give their job the best they have.

When all members of an organization strive for personal greatness and derive pride from the knowledge that their effort and performance contribute to the good of the group, you will unleash most powerful and productive forces.

Let the ambitious individual know that before advancing, they first must do their assigned role to the best of their ability. Let the overlooked individual better understand how their job benefits the team.

Remind those under your leadership that patience is required, and if they continue to improve, their chance will come, often when least expected. I cautioned ambitious players, "Be ready when your opportunity arrives or it may not arrive again."

COACH WOODEN'S X'S AND O'S:

MAKE GREATNESS AVAILABLE TO EVERYONE

- A leader's greatness is found in bringing out greatness in others.

- Personal greatness is measured—like success— against one's own potential, not that of someone else.

- Opportunity for advancement comes unexpectedly. Teach those you lead to be prepared for it when it happens. And be patient.

- Before calculus comes arithmetic. Advancement comes only with mastery of the assigned role and responsibility within the organization.

An effective leader is
very good at listening.
And it's difficult to listen
when you are talking.

LEADERSHIP LESSON #10:
SEEK SIGNIFICANT CHANGE

What I Learned

BY GARY CUNNINGHAM
UCLA VARSITY, 1960–62; ASSISTANT COACH, UCLA,
1966–75; HEAD COACH, UCLA, 1977, 1978.

John Wooden did not want "yes-men" around him. We were encouraged to argue our points, knowing he'd come back at us strong with his own opinions. That was his way of testing how much we believed in what we were telling him and how much we knew about it.

For example, we'd debate the pivot—what was the best way to do it—for 45 minutes during a morning meeting. But

he listened with an open mind, let us contribute—insisted on it. During those meetings, we didn't just sit and take notes. He wanted interaction, ideas back and forth. What changes can we make to improve our performance?

And he got it.

What It Means

Never make excuses. Your friends don't need them, and your foes won't believe them.

BY STEVE JAMISON

At the beginning of the 1961–62 season, John Wooden had been coaching basketball at UCLA for 12 years in conditions he describes as "harsh, perhaps as bad as any major university in the country."

The basketball facility at UCLA, the old Men's Gym, was an environment that prevented good teaching: crowded with other sports activities during his practices, badly ventilated, without an area where he could instruct the team privately, and so small the team had to play "home games" at local junior colleges.

When it came to assessing the possibility of winning a national championship, he felt there was no chance that UCLA would be able to go all the way. Too much was working against the Bruins. First and foremost, the "near-hardship" conditions at UCLA's gym diminished his potential for teaching.

How did this all affect his perspective as a coach? While circumspect in describing it, he suggests that perhaps it limited his thinking regarding the potential results available to his team in the national tournament. That is, winning a championship was not possible. However, events in the 1961–62 season changed his viewpoint completely, removed a subconscious barrier he may have imposed on himself, and set change in motion that would eventually produce 10 national championships and a basketball dynasty

What happened is a good lesson in how we can limit ourselves without even knowing it—how we can say "no" when we should be asking "how?"

In 1961–62 the UCLA Bruins advanced to the Final Four before losing in the final seconds to Cincinnati 72–70. A "phantom foul" for charging was called on the Bruins and Cincinnati gained possession of the ball and won the game.

Coach Wooden recognized that despite the primitive practice conditions at UCLA, the Bruins had come very close to winning a national championship.

This was a revelation. John Wooden recognized that it was time to seek significant change, to stop limiting his view of what the team might accomplish.

My Perspective | by John Wooden

Once I realized that the Men's Gym did not preclude winning a national championship, it seemed to open my mind, took the blinders off. I began an intense and comprehensive review of what I was doing and how I could do it better. I began searching for changes that would allow UCLA to consistently be more competitive in post-season play.

On the plane ride back from the tournament loss against Cincinnati in Louisville, assistant coach Jerry Norman began making his case as to why I should reconsider using a full court defense—the Press—in the upcoming season and beyond.

I listened carefully to what he said, even though I had heard and ignored it in previous years. This time, for reasons related to our near-win against Cincinnati—having the blinders removed from my eyes—I was really listening, and instead of saying "no" I said "yes." It was a significant change, and I made it.

The Press ultimately became a trademark of UCLA basketball and contributed to our run of championships.

It took UCLA's surprising appearance in the Final Four and a near-victory against Cincinnati for me to quit making excuses, to stop blaming the Men's Gym for our results. I'm pleased that it happened. I am not pleased that it was necessary.

> *Make each day*
> *your masterpiece.*

COACH WOODEN'S X'S AND O'S:

SEEK SIGNIFICANT CHANGE

- Never be content with performance or results.

- Remove all excuses for getting to the next level. Don't say "no"; ask "how?"

- A leader listens (especially to the leadership team).

- A robust exchange of ideas and opinions is healthy as long as it's done in a manner that is not disruptive or disrespectful.

LEADERSHIP LESSON #11: DON'T LOOK AT THE SCOREBOARD

What I Learned

BY DAVE MEYERS
UCLA VARSITY; 1973–75;
TWO NCAA NATIONAL CHAMPIONSHIPS

As a pro with the Milwaukee Bucks, absolutely nothing else mattered but winning. If you missed a shot or made a mistake, you were made to feel so terrible about it because all eyes were on the scoreboard.

On the other hand, Coach Wooden didn't talk about winning—never. His message was to give the practice the best you've got; give the game the best you've got. "That's the goal," he would tell us. "Do that and you are a success. If enough of you do it, our team will be a success." He teaches this, he believes it, and he taught me to believe it.

Winning was not mentioned—never—only the effort, the preparation, doing what it takes to bring out your best in practice and games. Let winning take care of itself. And it did.

What It Means

BY STEVE JAMISON

John Wooden kept a sealed envelope in his UCLA office that contained a slip of paper with predictions for game results on it for the upcoming season. Those predictions, filled in before the start of the season and filed away in a drawer, were as close as he came to worrying about what the scoreboard would show in future games; whether UCLA would beat some other team.

He wanted players to do likewise: to forget about the scoreboard and focus on doing their job at the highest possible level in practice and in competition. The score will take of itself. Focus on the present effort, not the future result.

An effective leader determines what occupies the organization's attention, what those individuals work on and worry about. This process begins with what you, the leader, are preoccupied with.

The scoreboard? Championships? A sales quota? The bottom line? As a day-to-day preoccupation, they're a waste of time because they steal attention and effort from the present and squander it on the future. You control the former, not the latter.

> *You can't do anything about yesterday, and the only way to improve tomorrow is by what you do right now.*

An organization—a team—that's always looking up at the scoreboard will find that a worthy opponent will steal the "ball" out from under you.

Coach Wooden's basic philosophy was to prepare for each opponent in the same way; respect all, fear none, and concentrate on teaching the Bruins to execute his system at their highest level. Teaching, learning, and execution are all done in the present moment. He says, "I didn't think that talking about winning all the time would increase our chances of doing so."

Thus, he never scouted other teams because he believed the Bruins were better off letting the opponent do the scouting and constant changing. He felt the players under his supervision would be stronger doing the same thing over and over—his system executed at the highest possible standard—than trying to change each week depending on who the opponent might be. There were exceptions to this, of course, but very few.

John Wooden focused almost entirely on improvement in the present moment. He let the score—winning—take care of itself.

Don't let yesterday take up too much of today.

My Perspective | by John Wooden

If you want to extend a winning streak, forget about it. If you want to break a losing streak, forget about it. Forget about everything except concentrating on the very hard work and intelligent planning necessary for never-ending improvement. Don't keep looking at the "scoreboard," the won-lost record, or the ongoing results in whatever form they may take. It removes your mind from the most important task, namely, figuring out how to improve the performance of your organization. Whether you are ahead or behind, on a winning streak or a losing streak, what matters most is your focus on improvement. The "scoreboard" in all its various forms is a siren that beckons, but only distracts and diminishes our attention to incessantly seeking ways to improve.

As the leader, my job was to help each player accomplish this, in part, by getting them to block out the future, the standings, or whatever they hoped the scoreboard might show at the end of a game.

It was a goal I never sealed in an envelope and filed away in my desk.

COACH WOODEN'S X'S AND O'S:

DON'T LOOK AT THE SCOREBOARD

- Worry about today's effort, not tomorrow's results.

- Watching the "scoreboard" is habit-forming. Break the habit.

- Define your dreams, hopes, and aspirations. Then file them away.

- Focus on running the race rather than winning it.

LEADERSHIP LESSON #12: ADVERSITY IS YOUR ASSET

What I Learned

BY KEN WASHINGTON
UCLA VARSITY, 1964–66; TWO NCAA NATIONAL
CHAMPIONSHIPS

The great lesson I take from Coach Wooden is this: the best thing you can do in life is your best. You're a winner when you do that even if you're on the short end of the score.

Too many factors can affect the final results; the fickle finger of fate can suddenly take over. The best talent doesn't always win, but the individual or team that goes out and

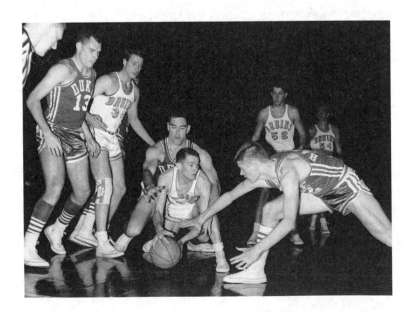

does their best is a winner. That's his philosophy. It's what he teaches.

We had a perfect season and won the national championship in 1964. We repeated as national champions in 1965. There was no question in my mind that in 1966 we could become the first team in college basketball history to win three championships in a row. Then the fickle finger of fate pointed at us.

Injuries, sickness, and all kinds of stuff were hitting us. We didn't even win our conference title in 1966—we had a 10–4 record and weren't even eligible to play in the NCAA tournament and defend our title.

> *Be a competitor. When the going gets tough, really get going.*

Through all of the misfortune, I never heard a single complaint or excuse from Coach Wooden. He fought hard and kept telling us to keep working, never give up, do our best. And we did in spite of the fickle finger of fate.

We were a success in 1966 because of that.

What It Means

BY STEVE JAMISON

Welcome adversity. It can make you stronger, better, tougher. Your competition will be tested too. The prize goes to the competitor who best deals with adversity. This starts by not blaming your troubles on bad luck. Blaming fate—bad luck—makes you weaker. Good things come only through adversity. Good leaders understand this.

Fate plays a role in leadership. Circumstances we neither foresee, understand, nor desire can be imposed without warning on us and our organizations in what seems to be a random fashion.

In trying times it is easy to feel the fates are working directly against you—to find an excuse to let up, lose heart, then quit.

You do not control the unwelcome twists and turns that are part of life and leadership. At those difficult moments, Coach Wooden drew strength from his father's strong example as well as his suggestion to worry only about those things over which you have control. We can't control fate, only our response to it.

Time and time again, fate intervened in his career. He believes the following: "Things turn out best for those who

> *Things turn out best for those who make the best of the way things turn out.*

make the best of the way things turn out." He did this in 1947 when a freak snowstorm prevented officials at the University of Minnesota from calling him to offer the head coaching job of the Minnesota Gophers. This was a job he wanted very much.

Instead, he went to UCLA and under "near-hardship conditions" won two national championships at the old Men's Gym, which led to eight more titles at Pauly Pavilion. Similarly, when the rules were changed, making the dunk illegal in college basketball and thus taking away a major offensive weapon available to

Kareem Abdul-Jabbar, Coach Wooden counseled him with this advice: "It can make you better, a more complete player." Result? Abdul-Jabbar's legendary sky-hook.

When knocked down by fate, a strong leader stands, takes a deep breath, and looks to make the best of the situation. They develop the ability to see adversity as usually offering a well-hidden blessing, an opportunity in disguise.

My Perspective | by John Wooden

Early on I had come to believe that events in life usually work out as they should, for a reason, even if that reason is not apparent. Perhaps it was because of my faith or the example of my parents. Perhaps because of my own experiences along the way. I don't know exactly why, but I began to better accept what fate seemed to offer and tried to make the very best of the situation, to move forward with optimism and the determination to make the most of the situation.

Those who prevail in a competitive environment look fate in the eye and say, "Welcome." Then they move ahead without complaint, excuse, or whining.

It is inevitable in leadership and in life that events occur that seem utterly incomprehensible and unfair. While we can't control fate, we can control how we react to the hand we're dealt.

In leadership, your reaction is crucial because the team will follow your example.

Be a realistic optimist and remind yourself that things turn out best for those who make the best of how things turn out.

COACH WOODEN'S X'S AND O'S:

ADVERSITY IS YOUR ASSET

- All leaders and their organizations are visited by misfortune and bad luck. You will not be the exception to the rule.

- "Woe is me" is not the theme song of an effective leader.

- Adversity makes us stronger, but only if we resist the temptation to blame fate for our troubles.

- How often have you not recognized an opportunity because it wore the disguise of bad luck?

Goals achieved with little effort
are seldom worthwhile or long-lasting.

COMPASS CHECK

✴ LEADERSHIP LESSON #1 ✴
GOOD VALUES ATTRACT GOOD PEOPLE

1. You are a leader. What are your top three core values as a leader?

_____

_____

_____

_____

_____

_____

_____

_____

_____

_____

_____

_____

_____

_____

_____

_____

_____

2. Describe three actions you will take to better communicate, make visible, and/or demonstrate your leadership values. Remember, you are a teacher rather than a "preacher." What is the difference?

_____

_____

_____

_____

_____

_____

_____

_____

_____

_____

_____

_____

_____

_____

_____

_____

_____

_____

_____

_____

3. List the top three characteristics, that is, values, you look for in a potential team member, and describe how you identify them in that individual and how you expect that candidate to identify them in you.

_____

_____

_____

_____

_____

_____

_____

_____

_____

_____

_____

_____

_____

_____

_____

_____

_____

_____

_____

✳ LEADERSHIP LESSON #2 ✳
USE THE MOST POWERFUL
FOUR-LETTER WORD

1. Describe your philosophy on personal relationships
   with team members as it compares with Coach
   Wooden's "extended family" approach.

   _____

   _____

   _____

   _____

   _____

   _____

   _____

   _____

   _____

   _____

   _____

   _____

   _____

   _____

   _____

   _____

   _____

   _____

   _____

2. List three actions—small gestures—you will take to demonstrate your "sincere care, concern, and consideration" for other team members.

_____

_____

_____

_____

_____

_____

_____

_____

_____

_____

_____

_____

_____

_____

_____

_____

_____

_____

_____

3. Describe a leader you have worked with in the past who demonstrated Coach Wooden's "extended family" perspective. Be specific in explaining the positive impact it had on you, how it was accomplished, and what application you might use in your own work.

_____

_____

_____

_____

_____

_____

_____

_____

_____

_____

_____

_____

_____

_____

_____

_____

✳ LEADERSHIP LESSON #3 ✳
CALL YOURSELF A TEACHER

1. Before you can teach, you must know what you want
   to teach. In general terms, describe what you are trying
   to teach in your leadership position.

   _____

   _____

   _____

   _____

   _____

   _____

   _____

   _____

   _____

   _____

   _____

   _____

   _____

   _____

   _____

   _____

   _____

   _____

2. Describe your greatest asset as a leader/teacher and
   your greatest weakness.

_____

_____

_____

_____

_____

_____

_____

_____

_____

_____

_____

_____

_____

_____

_____

_____

_____

_____

_____

_____

_____

3. What three actions will you take to improve your teaching? (For example, convening a monthly "open forum" where those on your team can ask questions and learn from your experience.)

_____

_____

_____

_____

_____

_____

_____

_____

_____

_____

_____

_____

_____

_____

_____

_____

_____

_____

✳ LEADERSHIP LESSON #4 ✳
EMOTION IS YOUR ENEMY

1. John Wooden teaches that intensity is productive and emotionalism counterproductive. Explain how Coach Wooden defines and distinguishes these two important behaviors, and reflect on your own perspective vis-à-vis these behaviors.

_____

_____

_____

_____

_____

_____

_____

_____

_____

_____

_____

_____

_____

_____

_____

_____

_____

2. Recall an occasion on which you went from intensity to emotionalism. Describe what caused your "temperature" to go up and what you did or would do to prevent the escalation from recurring.

_____

_____

_____

_____

_____

_____

_____

_____

_____

_____

_____

_____

_____

_____

_____

_____

_____

_____

3. Self-Control, especially in the context of emotions, but not limited to it, is a John Wooden fundamental for Success. Identify those areas of your performance and behavior that typically lack solid discipline, structure, or self-will. Describe what actions you would take to improve.

_____

_____

_____

_____

_____

_____

_____

_____

_____

_____

_____

_____

_____

_____

_____

_____

_____

_____

_____

✳ LEADERSHIP LESSON #5 ✳
IT TAKES 10 HANDS
TO SCORE A BASKET

1. Describe a situation in which you or someone on the team was not a "10 hands" team member and put self-interest ahead of the interests of the group. Describe a situation when the opposite occurred.

_____

_____

_____

_____

_____

_____

_____

_____

_____

_____

_____

_____

_____

_____

_____

_____

2. What was the best "10 hands" team you were ever on, and what lessons from that experience will you seek to incorporate in the weeks ahead?

_____

_____

_____

_____

_____

_____

_____

_____

_____

_____

_____

_____

_____

_____

_____

_____

_____

_____

_____

_____

_____

_____

3. Describe in detail three actions you will implement to encourage others to "share the ball"—information, ideas, and opportunities.

_____

_____

_____

_____

_____

_____

_____

_____

_____

_____

_____

_____

_____

_____

_____

_____

_____

_____

_____

_____

✳ LEADERSHIP LESSON #6 ✳
LITTLE THINGS MAKE
BIG THINGS HAPPEN

1. Describe a failure "on your watch" that resulted from sloppy attention to details.

_____

_____

_____

_____

_____

_____

_____

_____

_____

_____

_____

_____

_____

_____

_____

_____

_____

_____

2. List three areas of "details" that you will focus on with
greater emphasis in the weeks ahead. Describe how
you will teach this habit of caring about details to your
team.

_____

_____

_____

_____

_____

_____

_____

_____

_____

_____

_____

_____

_____

_____

_____

_____

_____

_____

3. Identify a detail that John Wooden stressed that has application in your leadership. Describe how you will incorporate it. [For a complete description of his assiduous identification and perfection of details, refer to *Wooden on Leadership* (McGraw-Hill).]

_____

_____

_____

_____

_____

_____

_____

_____

_____

_____

_____

_____

_____

_____

_____

_____

_____

_____

_____

✳ LEADERSHIP LESSON #7 ✳
MAKE EACH DAY YOUR MASTERPIECE

1. List several "Coach Quotes" to share with your team. What would be some appropriate opportunities to remind and reinforce their meaning to your team? What relevant quotes are there from other leaders you respect? What can be incorporated into your teaching?

_____

_____

_____

_____

_____

_____

_____

_____

_____

_____

_____

_____

_____

_____

2. By his description, John Wooden was as good as any
   coach in the country in his management/organization
   of time. Analyze your own management of time.
   Describe in detail how you can improve specific areas.

_____

_____

_____

_____

_____

_____

_____

_____

_____

_____

_____

_____

_____

_____

_____

_____

_____

_____

_____

3. Reflect in a meaningful manner on the responsibilities and trust incumbent on you as a leader. Ask yourself, "In what specific ways am I honoring this trust?" Ask yourself, "In what ways have I fallen short of creating 'a masterpiece' in my leadership?"

✳ LEADERSHIP LESSON #8 ✳
THE CARROT IS MIGHTIER
THAN A STICK

1. Identify a number of instances when you have offered praise or criticism. Give thought to the ratio of praise to criticism as well as the total number of instances. What are your conclusions?

_____

_____

_____

_____

_____

_____

_____

_____

_____

_____

_____

_____

_____

_____

_____

_____

_____

2. The "carrot" is powerful. List current and new creative "carrots" you will incorporate in your leadership methodology.

_____

_____

_____

_____

_____

_____

_____

_____

_____

_____

_____

_____

_____

_____

_____

_____

_____

_____

_____

_____

_____

3. Describe how you might create a monthly Pyramid of
   Success award for a team member who best exhibits
   a specific characteristic you have selected (e.g.,
   Initiative).

   _____

   _____

   _____

   _____

   _____

   _____

   _____

   _____

   _____

   _____

   _____

   _____

   _____

   _____

   _____

   _____

   _____

   _____

   _____

   _____

✳ LEADERSHIP LESSON #9 ✳
MAKE GREATNESS AVAILABLE
TO EVERYONE

1. Evaluate your actions and effectiveness in teaching
   each member of your team the importance of the
   individual's job as it pertains to the group's success—
   especially for those in lesser roles.

   _____

   _____

   _____

   _____

   _____

   _____

   _____

   _____

   _____

   _____

   _____

   _____

   _____

   _____

2. Identify deserving team members who have achieved
   Competitive Greatness at work. What do you think
   their performance perspectives on doing their job
   would be?

_____

_____

_____

_____

_____

_____

_____

_____

_____

_____

_____

_____

_____

_____

_____

_____

_____

_____

_____

3. Using Coach Wooden's 12 Lessons in Leadership, identify and discuss a personalized "lesson" that you could share with your team on a monthly basis. Describe how you will make each lesson a reality; include specific examples as to how this lesson can be put to good use by you and your team during each particular month.

✳ LEADERSHIP LESSON #10 ✳
SEEK SIGNIFICANT CHANGE

1. Describe a plan that will encourage and reward team
   members for input, even "out of the box" ideas.

   _____

   _____

   _____

   _____

   _____

   _____

   _____

   _____

   _____

   _____

   _____

   _____

   _____

   _____

   _____

   _____

   _____

   _____

   _____

   _____

2. How will you create opportunities for "brain-storming" sessions in which current practices, behaviors, and more are examined and improved.

_____

_____

_____

_____

_____

_____

_____

_____

_____

_____

_____

_____

_____

_____

_____

_____

_____

_____

3. List three leaders you will contact in the next several months with an eye toward gaining insights into their leadership philosophy and methodology.

_____

_____

_____

_____

_____

_____

_____

_____

_____

_____

_____

_____

_____

_____

_____

_____

_____

_____

_____

_____

_____

_____

✳ LEADERSHIP LESSON #11 ✳
DON'T LOOK AT THE SCOREBOARD

1. John Wooden virtually removed the "final score" as the final goal. Describe how you can incorporate his philosophy into your own job and convey it to those with whom you work.

_____

_____

_____

_____

_____

_____

_____

_____

_____

_____

_____

_____

_____

_____

2. Coach Wooden found his greatest joy in the journey, the day-to-day process of improvement. Describe your own perspective on the process. Write down a summary of where you find the joy in your professional journey. What in Coach Wooden's perspective can you bring into your own approach?

_____

_____

_____

_____

_____

_____

_____

_____

_____

_____

_____

_____

_____

_____

_____

_____

_____

_____

_____

3. Discuss three actions you would take to increase
   team focus on improvement while diminishing in a
   productive manner constant "scoreboard" checking.

⁂ LEADERSHIP LESSON #12 ⁂
ADVERSITY IS YOUR ASSET

1. Give an example of a setback, accident, or failure that was turned into an advantage. What did you learn from the experience?

_____

_____

_____

_____

_____

_____

_____

_____

_____

_____

_____

_____

_____

_____

_____

_____

_____

_____

2. Create a step-by-step formula for responding to
   setbacks, losses, or poor performance that ensures
   a measured and productive response.

3. Examine your personal experiences for examples of "adversity becomes an asset." What patterns, if any, do you discern, and how can you incorporate them in the future?

_____

_____

_____

_____

_____

_____

_____

_____

_____

_____

_____

_____

_____

_____

_____

_____

_____

_____

_____

_____

PART IV

REFLECTIONS ON LEADERSHIP

50 MAXIMS AND OBSERVATIONS
ON LEADERSHIP

Ability may get you to the top,
but it takes character to stay there.

> Leaders often change when success arrives. Some be-
> gin to believe that what got them to the top is enough
> to stay there. It isn't. Complacency is a character issue.

When you're through
learning, you're through.

> Learning is a leader's lifetime pursuit. You must never
> reach the point of self-delusion that suggests you know
> it all. Remind yourself, "It's what I learn after I know it
> all that counts." It's the truth.

The journey is better than the inn.

> Cervantes, with those words, sums up my perspective on
> trophies, championships, and other "rewards"; namely,
> they are secondary—a by-product of the journey itself,
> the process of striving for personal greatness. For me,
> a victory on the court—"being better than someone

else"—can be satisfying. What precedes it, however, can bring joy and the greatest self-satisfaction. The joys of the journey exceed the comforts of the inn.

It's important to keep trying to do what you think is right, no matter how hard it is or how often you fail. You never stop trying.

If you're not making mistakes, you're not doing anything.

Coach "Piggy" Lambert told me at Purdue University, "The team that makes the most mistakes probably wins." The doer makes mistakes. However, be sure your mistakes are not the result of poor preparation or sloppy execution. Winners make the right kind of mistakes.

Do not let what you can't do interfere with what you can do.

When you allow yourself to get caught up in things over which you have no control, it affects those things over which you do have control. Time is limited. Focus on that which you can improve, correct, or change. Ignore what you can't control.

Failure to act is often the biggest failure of all.

"Tentative" is a word I do not associate with Competitive Greatness. The leader who is afraid to face failure will seldom face Success. You must have the courage to make a decision and then execute expeditiously.

Little things make big things happen.

Success is built from the ground up. I showed players how to put their sweat socks on correctly. Small things—laughable to some—are connected to big things such as a national championship. The particulars may differ for you and your team, but success is built from the bottom up.

The best way to improve the team is to improve yourself.

We become so intent on improving the performance level of others that we neglect our own shortcomings. Honest self-evaluation is the first and often most difficult step in a leader's own improvement.

You are not a failure until you start blaming others for your mistakes.

Time spent complaining is time wasted. The leader is responsible for the team's performance. The moment you seek to set responsibility on the doorstep of another, you have deluded yourself. Self-delusion is self-destruction.

The force of character is cumulative.

Those words by Ralph Waldo Emerson can be put this way: "Birds of a feather flock together." A leader with character attracts people with character. They become a team that is formidable under fire.

> *"For maximum team accomplishment, each individual must prepare himself to the best of his ability and then put his talent to work for the team. This must be done unselfishly, without thought of personal glory. When no one worries about who will receive the credit, far more can be accomplished in any group activity."*
> —PRESEASON LETTER TO THE TEAM, 1964

The main ingredient of stardom is the rest of the team.

I'm asked, "Coach Wooden, how did you win all those championships?" My response is factual: "I didn't win all those championships. Our team did." In 27 years at UCLA, I didn't score a single basket. My job was to help others do it. The star of the team is your team.

Nobody cares how much you know until they know how much you care.

Care, concern, and a sincere consideration for those in your organization is the mark of a strong leader. These traits do not make you appear weak, soft, or vulnerable. On the contrary, they are perceived by those you lead as a sign of self-confidence. Be confident enough to care. And to show it.

Don't mistake activity for achievement.

To produce results, tasks must be well organized and properly executed; otherwise, it's no different from children running around the playground—everybody is doing something, but nothing is being done; lots of activity, no achievement.

Discipline yourself and others won't need to.

Some leaders find it easier to enforce rules and regulations on others than on themselves. How can you control your team if you can't control yourself? A team with discipline begins with a well-disciplined leader. I've never seen it work the opposite way.

"Love" is the greatest word in the English language. "Balance" is the second-greatest word.

Body balance is crucial for a basketball player. Emotional balance is crucial for everyone. Balance in life is necessary for optimal performance in leadership. 24/7 is necessary on occasion, but as a way of life, it means you're out of balance. Someone or something that is out of balance is likely to fall over and break.

> *"I must caution you that you cannot live in the past. The 1971–72 season is now history, and we must look toward the future. The past cannot change what is to come. The work that you do each and every day is the only true way to improve and prepare yourself for what is to come. You cannot change the past, but you can influence the future by what you do today."*
> —PRESEASON LETTER TO THE TEAM, 1972

A leader has one team, not "starters" and "substitutes."

I tried hard to avoid cliques or any kind of caste system at UCLA. If a starter referred to a nonstarter as a "sub," he'd be on the bench. The "sub" would have his job while the starter learned his lesson. Favoritism is fatal.

Failing to prepare is preparing to fail.

My definition of success states that you must make the utmost effort to bring forth your talent. This is how you prepare to win. Do otherwise and you are simply preparing to fail.

If you have done your job in preparing the team, the team is prepared to do its job in playing the game. So let them.

I honestly felt that if I'd been successful in my teaching at practice during the week, I could watch the game from the stands on Saturday and the players would do just fine. Teach your team what to do, and then let them do it.

Be quick, but don't hurry.

Expect hustle from those under your supervision, but caution them not to expedite at a pace that increases the chance of errors. I prize quickness in execution of tasks, but not a pace so hurried that mistakes are likely.

No written word nor spoken plea can teach your team what it should be.

The most effective teaching tool is the power of your example—for better or worse. A leader who exhibits hustle, efficiency, fairness, courage, skill, and other positive characteristics will see that reflected in the organization. Of course, some of those on the team won't reflect these things. You must then do the right thing: help them find another team.

The past cannot change what is to come. The work that you do each and every day is the only true way to improve and prepare yourself for what is to come. You cannot change the past, and you can only influence the future by what you do today.

—Preseason Letter to the Team, 1968

Perfection of relevant details is silly to some, but it's not funny to me.

Races are won by a fraction of a second; national championship games by a single point. That fraction of a second or single point is the result of relevant details perfected along the way. Leave nothing to chance. The difference between the championship team and a merely good team is the perfection and execution of relevant details. Sloppiness breeds sloppiness.

The infection of success is often fatal.

Most people work harder on the way to the top than when they arrive. If you're fortunate enough to get there, do not be swayed. Allow success to turn your head and you'll be looking failure right in the face.

More often than we ever suspect, the lives of others we do affect.

Leadership is a trust—a sacred trust, in my opinion. It goes beyond meeting quotas or winning a basketball game. You have the opportunity to change a person's life by helping him or her become the best he or she is capable of becoming.

Define "normal" as "abnormally high."

The list was entitled "Normal Expectations." It included "Never waste time"; "Never be selfish, jealous, envious, or egotistical"; "Keep emotions under control without losing fight or aggressiveness"; "Work constantly to improve without becoming satisfied"; "Never expect favors"; "Never have reason to be sorry afterward"; "Acquire peace of mind by becoming the best that you are capable of becoming"; "Be on time"; and more. These were just my normal expectations for those under my supervision.

Play to win, but play fair.

Is there a difference between robbing a bank for money and breaking the rules to win? Neither means much except to a thief. Cheating to win doesn't make you a winner. How you play the game does count—at least to me. Don't envy those with ill-gotten gains, whether it be money, fame, or victory.

You must discipline yourself to do what is expected of you for the welfare of the team. The coach has many decisions to make, and you will not agree with all of them, but you must respect and accept them. Without supervision and leadership and a disciplined effort by all, much of our united strength will be dissipated pulling against ourselves. Let us not be victimized by a breakdown from within.
—PRESEASON LETTER TO THE TEAM, 1965

The will to win means nothing without the will to work.

I told those under my supervision, "Don't tell me what you will do. Show me." Talking about hard work is a lot easier than working hard. I sought individuals who played "tall" more than individuals who were tall.

You cannot antagonize and influence at the same time.

Leadership involves the task of influencing others in a positive way: first of all, those on your team. How can you accomplish this if you annoy, irritate, and alienate those you wish to influence? I was often critical of players, but I tried hard to avoid personal attacks, embarrassment, or demeaning comments, which would make them less likely to take my criticism to heart.

Learn as if you were to live forever; live as if you were to die tomorrow.

Be voracious in your daily desire to acquire knowledge, information, and wisdom. Be joyful and appreciative of the blessing of this day you've been given.

Happiness begins where selfishness ends.

Selflessness is the start of a happy team. Individual statistics have value only in regard to how they benefit the group. A team member who hoards information, contacts, knowledge, the "ball"—at the expense of the group—hurts the group.

Fear is short-term; pride lasts.

Instilling fear is a quick and easy way to motivate someone. It won't last for long with talented people. Create pride with meaningful praise, sincere interest, and selfless dedication to the team. Fear has a place. Pride has first place.

*If I do not feel there is a place where you can contribute,
I would not want to waste your time, and if you do not feel
that you are part of the team as a whole, then you should
drop out. Although I prefer to go too far with a play
rather than not far enough, I will drop you when I feel
certain that you are wasting your time."*
—PRESEASON LETTER TO THE TEAM, 1967

There is no such thing as an overachiever.

Regardless of our individual talent, we're all under-achievers to different degrees. In 40 years of coaching, I never asked a player to give me 110 percent. I always held to the belief that 100 percent was plenty. In fact, it was everything.

Do not be vulnerable to praise or criticism from outsiders.

Your strength of consistency depends on how you let praise and criticism affect you. Some of it will be deserved and some of it will be undeserved. Either way, don't get caught up in the opinions of others. When you are honest in your self-analysis, your opinion should count the most.

If you don't have time to do it right, when will you have time to do it over?

In a competitive environment, you will face an overwhelming number of issues that need to be dealt with right now. Thus, it is easy to get sloppy, to give less than total attention to the task at hand. It is better to do one thing correctly than ten poorly. Don't be the leader who gets a lot done, but nothing done well.

I will get ready, and then, perhaps, my chance will come.

Those under my supervision were cautioned to prepare for the chance to prove themselves: "Be ready and your opportunity may come. But if you're not ready, it may not come again." The same applies to those who aspire to higher levels of leadership. You must prepare before opportunity knocks. It seldom knocks twice.

Be more interested in finding the best way, not in having it your way.

A healthy ego—necessary in leadership—often inflates. You suddenly have all the answers and say, "It's my way or the highway." When this occurs, you'll find some very talented people in your organization taking the highway just because they couldn't get a fair hearing.

> *There is much truth in Kipling's "Law of the Jungle" where he says, "The strength of the pack is the wolf, and the strength of the wolf is the pack." If you discipline yourself toward team effort under the supervision of the coach, even though you may not always agree with my decisions, much can and will be accomplished. As someone once said, "You will be amazed at how much can be accomplished if no one cares who gets the credit."*
> —PRESEASON LETTER TO THE TEAM, 1927

Make sure those under your supervision feel they are working with you, not for you.

"All for one and one for all" also applies to the leader. At UCLA, I sincerely believed we were all working together—the players, the assistant coaches, the trainer, the managers. For best results, everyone must feel they are working with everyone else. Seek the right way, not just having it your way.

Goals achieved with little effort are seldom worthwhile or long-lasting.

When nothing is at stake, few compete or care for the results. Take comfort when the field is crowded with worthy opponents. It means you're in a battle that matters. A great competitor loves the hard battle. Only the worthy opponent brings out your best.

Come in and talk to me whenever you feel like it, but please remember that it isn't necessarily lack of communication if we fail to agree on your position or another individual on the team. I am and will always be interested in your problems, but I do feel that everyone should do everything possible to work out their own problems rather than become dependent upon others. I have found prayer most helpful when I am troubled, and I believe that all prayers are heard and answered, even though the answer may be "no."

—Preseason Letter to the Team, 1972

Time spent getting even is best spent getting ahead.

"Sharp elbows" in basketball means a player is overly aggressive, throwing his elbows around. The player who gets hit in the head and tries to retaliate is usually called for the foul. "Forget it," I would say in practice. "Get even by scoring." Regardless of who's throwing the "elbows," it's tough to forget about it when you get hit. Get even by winning.

There is nothing stronger than gentleness.

Dictator-style leaders rule by fear and force, humiliation and intimidation. These are the same "leadership" tools used by a prison guard. You achieve better results with talented people when you treat them like human beings. The most powerful motivator is a compliment from someone you respect. It's true for you, and it's true for those under your supervision.

Be slow to criticize. Be quick to commend.

Many leaders find it easier to be negative than positive, to criticize rather than commend. It's just a bad habit. However, when criticism was necessary, as it often was, I tried to say something positive first—then the criticism. I believe the greatest motivator is a pat on the back, although sometimes that "pat" must be a little lower and a little harder.

Much more can be accomplished when no one is concerned about who gets credit.

Selflessness means putting others—the team and its goals—first, ahead of one's own glory or statistics. It's among the most valuable qualities an individual can bring to the team. If a player didn't come by it naturally, I taught them how. The bench was my teaching tool.

Agree to disagree without being disagreeable.

The path to improvement has enough obstacles. A leader makes it more difficult by being surly, contentious, and disagreeable. Control this in yourself; prohibit it in others. A bad attitude is contagious.

You must earn the right to be proud and confident.

On the occasion when UCLA had won a national championship the preceding year, I would start the new season off with these words: "Do not feel that anything that happened last year should have any bearing on this year. You must establish your own identity." I wanted them to understand clearly that they could not assume the championship identity of the previous team. They had to earn it themselves.

Give credit to those who do little jobs in a big way.

Everybody likes some attention. In basketball or business, there are big producers who get all the notice and acclaim. At press conferences, I countered this by directing attention to those who helped the "big producer" produce so much. A leader is wise to remember that a big producer is assisted by a big team.

You can't make up for poor effort today by working harder tomorrow.

We kid ourselves: "I'll buckle down to business tomorrow and work twice as hard." No. If you can work "twice as hard" tomorrow, it means you've been holding something back, not giving 100 percent today. I want 100 percent today and tomorrow.

My experience in teaching and coaching over many years has naturally caused me to become somewhat opinionated in certain areas, but even most of those who are inexperienced will agree that experience is a great, although sometimes hard, teacher."
—PRESEASON LETTER TO THE TEAM, 1967

Heed this observation: "Others, too, have brains."

A leader listens. Don't act like you're listening when you're just waiting to talk. People know when you're not hearing what they say. Sometimes we forget that we're not the only smart person in the room.

Don't measure yourself by what you've accomplished, but by what you should have accomplished with your abilities.

The contest is within, to bring out your best. That's the ultimate challenge and responsibility. Measure your success on the basis of how close you got to realizing your full potential.

Consider the rights of others before your own feelings, and the feelings of others before your own rights.

Consideration for the rights and feelings of others is a small price to pay for the great goodwill that will be returned to you.

The smallest good deed is better than the biggest intention.

The greatest gift means nothing if it's not given. Don't let procrastination make you its partner in doing nothing.

A leader must have courage, including the courage to change.

We must fight for what we believe in—up to a point. Remember this bit of verse: "Stubbornness we deprecate / Firmness we condone / The former is my neighbor's trait / The latter is my own."

Things turn out best for those who make the best of the way things turn out.

The ancient proverb says, "Crisis presents opportunity." It is the opportunity to dig deeper and rise higher; to get stronger and be smarter; to find a better way, a different path. Adversity offers the opportunity, but you must recognize it.

It has been almost four months since our basketball season came to a close. It was a very successful season [UCLA had won its sixth national championship in seven years], but it is now history and we must look toward the future. The past cannot change what is to come. It is what you do today that counts, and I sincerely hope that you are looking forward to an outstanding 1970–71 season and are eager, not just willing, to make the necessary personal sacrifices to reach that goal. All worthwhile accomplishments require sacrifice and hard work."
—PRESEASON LETTER TO THE TEAM, 1970

PART V

A LEADERSHIP REALITY CHECK

YOU WILL MAKE NO PROGRESS
WITHOUT SELF-AWARENESS.

1. As a leader, what is the most gratifying praise you could hear from a member of your team?

_____

_____

_____

_____

_____

_____

> *Be slow to criticize and quick to commend.*

2. What criticism of your leadership would be most painful to hear?

_____

_____

_____

_____

_____

3. What aspect of leadership do you love the most?

_____

_____

_____

_____

_____

4. What is your greatest fear as a leader?

_____

_____

_____

_____

_____

> *The best way to improve the team is to improve yourselves.*

5. What single characteristic do you possess as a leader that someone would be well-served to emulate? Your most valuable asset?

_____

_____

_____

_____

_____

6. What characteristic do you exhibit that a potential leader would be wise to avoid?

_____

_____

_____

_____

_____

_____

7. If you wrote a book about your life and leadership, what would the title be? And the subtitle?

_____

_____

_____

_____

_____

_____

8. To this point, what is your greatest achievement as a leader?

_____

_____

_____

_____

_____

_____

9. What single personal asset would you like to acquire as part of your leadership skill set?

_____

_____

_____

_____

_____

10. Which leader—outside of your company—do you identify with?

_____

_____

_____

_____

_____

11. What trait do you most deplore in individuals?

_____

_____

_____

_____

_____

12. What trait do you most dislike in yourself as a leader?

_____

_____

_____

_____

_____

13. What is the most overrated virtue associated with leaders?

_____

_____

_____

_____

_____

14. What is the most underrated characteristic associated with leadership?

_____

_____

_____

_____

_____

> *Time spent getting*
> *even would be better spent*
> *trying to get ahead.*

15. What is your greatest regret as a leader?

_____

_____

_____

_____

_____

16. What part of leadership do you dislike most?

_____

_____

_____

_____

17. If you could change one thing you did as a leader, what would it be?

_____

_____

_____

_____

18. What is your response to team failure—coming up short?

_____

_____

_____

_____

19. If you were to die and come back as a leader in any occupation—business, military, religion, education, or otherwise—what would it be and why?

_____

_____

_____

_____

> *Ability may get you to the top,*
> *but it takes character to stay there.*

20. Which sports leader, present company excluded, do you most admire and why?

_____

_____

_____

_____

_____

21. What, if anything, is inhibiting or stopping you from becoming the kind of leader you envision yourself being?

_____

_____

_____

_____

_____

22. What is your definition of failure?

_____

_____

_____

_____

23. What is your definition of success?

_____

_____

_____

_____

_____

24. What do you consider the four most important
    values for leadership?

_____

_____

_____

_____

_____

25. What do you consider the four most important
    values in those you lead?

_____

_____

_____

_____

_____

PART VI

WOODEN'S TEAM

COACH WOODEN'S
FIELD OF DREAMS

KAREEM ABDUL-JABBAR: UCLA VARSITY, 1967–69;
THREE NCAA NATIONAL CHAMPIONSHIPS

You may have seen the Kevin Costner movie *Field of Dreams*—"Build it and they will come." Coach Wooden did that. He built his basketball program a certain way—athletically, ethically, morally—because he believed it would attract a certain type of person, the kind of individual he wanted on the team.

And if he didn't have success that way, it was all right with him because he felt his program made sense; in every way it made sense to him. So he was going to do it that way. Coach was almost a mystic in knowing what would happen. And, he was right—when he built it, they came. I was one of them.

I chose UCLA in large part because of what I saw and heard regarding those values. Dr. Ralph Bunche and Jackie Robinson wrote to me saying UCLA was a great place for an education and athletics. Willie Naulls told me that race wasn't an issue with Coach Wooden.

And one of the most important things in my decision was seeing Rafer Johnson on the *Ed Sullivan Show*. I knew he was a world-class athlete, but he was on the show as president of the student body at UCLA. That told me the school appreciated him for more than just being a jock. It told me a whole lot about what UCLA was about.

With his hair parted in the middle, Coach looked like he fell off a box of Pepperidge Farm cookies. That was misleading. In the gym he was a very, very tough man, extremely demanding. He wanted it done a certain way, and he would get out there and demonstrate what that way was.

Coach was about 57 years old when I arrived at UCLA— almost 40 years older than the rest of us. But he would never ask his players to do what he wouldn't do. You appreciate that, when the leader is willing to get right out there and work alongside you. You're not just hearing stuff from somebody who hasn't been there and done it. He knew what he was talking about, so he had that credibility. He got respect.

Winning was never mentioned by him. For Coach Wooden it was, "Fellas, we've got to play at our best. Let's do that." That's a lot different from saying, "Fellas, we've got to win." A lot different.

Race? Religion? They didn't matter. What mattered was the effort you made on the court and in the classroom. What mattered was your behavior, your conduct, your values. Of course, that included a strong work ethic.

He wanted our best effort. If that wasn't good enough, he accepted the results. Coach Wooden figured maybe that's the way it's supposed to be. But he wanted our best effort before he'd be willing to say, "That's the way it's supposed to be."

By the second week of practice at UCLA, I was just totally hooked on how he did things—the progression of skills he had us work on and then putting it all together as a team.

When they outlawed the dunk, he told me, "Lewis, everybody will be playing under the same rules no matter what they are. This game isn't about the dunk shot. So just go on and play; it's the same for everybody." Very matter of fact. Mentally, I got past the rule change outlawing the dunk shot very quickly.

One of his strongest assets as a leader was his patience. A lot of players were skeptical about various things, and it would take a while to win them over. Coach would let them try it their way and fail. He was good at that. It's the best way to teach. Because after they failed, they wanted to know how to do it right. They wanted to learn how to do it right more than they wanted to prove Coach wrong.

So, here's this 57-year-old guy, and he gets out there and shows them how to do it right.

He knew how to do it right—in all departments.

KEEP LISTENING; KEEP LEARNING; KEEP TEACHING

DENNY CRUM: UCLA VARSITY, 1958–59;
ASSISTANT COACH, 1969–71; THREE NATIONAL
CHAMPIONSHIPS

Coach Wooden's teaching was so effective because he was so well organized with his details. Everything was written out on the 3×5 cards and in notebooks: what was happening from 3:07 to 3:11; what we'd do from 3:11 to 3:17; who was doing what when. Nothing was left to chance; every minute was accounted for—every single minute.

And he was extremely disciplined in keeping to the schedule. I saw that when I was his assistant coach, and I saw it when I arrived at UCLA as a player. He taught details.

On my first day of practice, Coach Wooden sat us down and told the players to take off our sneakers and socks. He did the same. Then he went through his careful demonstration showing us how to eliminate wrinkles, creases, and folds in our sweat socks. We'd usually wear two pair of socks, and he showed how to smooth them out one pair at a time; tuck 'em in from the toe on down, kind of squeeze out the wrinkles and folds. Very precise. He wanted those socks to be smoothed out all the way up the calves.

There were some funny looks around me, but Coach was not willing to take any chances on details he deemed important to performance. So he taught us how to do it right.

That attention to detail was in *everything* he did—the way he planned practice, ran practice, evaluated practice and games. It applied to details of travel, equipment, and food. Absolutely everything that could affect performance got taken care of.

Here's something else that set him apart from 99 percent of the other coaches: Coach Wooden never thought he knew everything. In spite of the fact that he'd been winning championships every year—four or five of them when I got there as an assistant coach—he wanted to keeping learning, improving as a coach and leader.

I had spent a few years coaching at the junior college level when I joined him as an assistant in 1968. I brought with me some experience and my own ideas—which he welcomed. Those he liked we put in during practice. If they worked, fine. If not, we took it out.

He never thought his way was the only way. He continued like that right up to his final game. We used to have disagreements, really argue over things, and people would ask him about it. Coach would say, "I don't need 'yes-men.' If they're going to yes everything I do, I don't need them around."

When I came up with an idea, he would never tell me, "Well, this is the way we've always done it and we're winning championships. So, no, I'm not changing." He was open to change.

His approach was to listen; if he thought it made sense, try it. If it works, great. If not, move on. He was always searching for ways to improve.

In the daily coaches' meetings there was never an interruption from outside. We would have out our notebooks, evaluate the previous day's practice—what worked, what needed more work, what to do that was new. Adjustments and refinements.

Then we started formatting the practice minute to minute: a change-of-pace drill; change-of-direction drill; defensive sliding drill; reverse pivot on the dribble drill—on and on and on. We'd put it down in notebooks and on cards.

But through it all there was a wide-open flow of ideas and opinions. He was open to suggestion and contrary thoughts, but he was tough. You had to know your stuff to convince him to change. He never did something on a whim. You had to have your reasons in place, but he'd let you have your say.

Then, when everyone had had their say, he made the decision. And that was it.

Coach Wooden never talked about the winning or the losing. It was never part of the conversation like you would think is normal. He wouldn't come in before a game and say, "This team is tied with us in the conference, so we've got to step it up tonight. Let's win this one."

He just wasn't concerned about the opponents and what they might be up to—didn't even scout most of them. His philosophy was to do what was necessary to make UCLA a better team. Teach it; practice it. The details and the fundamentals were his main concern.

He just was completely absorbed in improvement for our team without trying to always be adjusting to what another team might be up to. "Let them adjust to us," he said.

Fundamentals, condition, play together as a team. That's all he did—simple as that. So simple.

A COOL LEADER
PREVENTS OVERHEATING

Fred Slaughter: UCLA varsity, 1962–64;
one national championship

I think there were four or five games in my career at UCLA when we started out behind something like 18–2—just getting killed. I'd look over at Coach Wooden, and there he'd sit on the bench with his program rolled up in his hand—totally unaffected, almost like we were ahead. And I'd think to myself, "Hey, if he's not worried, why should I be worried? Let's just do what the guy told us to do."

And you know what? We won all those games except one, and even that was close. It's the doggonest experience to see that. He was cool when it counted; his confidence and strength became ours. In my three years on the UCLA varsity team, I never once saw him rattled.

Coach Wooden dealt in the positive. He would not spend time on the negative—he was always focusing on moving forward with what we had to learn to make us better.

He could sense when we might be thinking negatively, getting down on ourselves. Then he'd come in all positive: "This is what you guys are supposed to do. Follow this and we'll be fine." No browbeating or yelling. And after a while we'd look back and, doggone, we were fine. Coach Wooden had his system, and he believed in it, and he taught us to believe in it.

He'd keep telling us, "Focus on what I'm teaching. Don't focus on the score. Just do what you're supposed to do and things will work out fine. Just play as a team and we'll be fine." He was always supportive, even when he was correcting something wrong.

Most of all he taught us unity and oneness of purpose in what we were doing, namely, working to be the very best we could be—to perform our best out there on the court.

And he understood how to get you to listen. When I arrived at UCLA, I was shooting a fade-away jump shot, and it was good. I used it in high school to become the number-one high school player in Kansas. But Coach Wooden didn't like it. He told me, "Fred, you know what I want is when you're finished with the shot to be around the basket. We need you to rebound. Now, if you fade away, you remove yourself from rebounding."

But I loved that shot. I wouldn't give it up until I heard him say very calmly, "Fred, you can do it the way I am teaching you or you can watch the game next Saturday sitting next to me on the bench. Your replacement knows how to shoot the jump shot correctly."

Oh my goodness, I've got to tell you, you don't understand the impact of that statement. And he didn't have to throw a chair across the floor to get his point across to me.

We lost to Cincinnati in the semifinals of the national championship because of a bad charging call on us during the last minute of the game. It was a phantom call, and it cost UCLA the game and maybe the national championship. Coach's reaction in the locker room was the same as if we'd won—cool. No complaining; he told us to keep our heads up: "Adversity makes us stronger." And then he said, "Remember, you've still got one another."

But he should have added, "and you've still got me." He was part of us. He was out on the court with us even when he was sitting on the bench. And, he was right about adversity. It made us stronger. Two years later, UCLA won its first NCAA national championship.

SHARE THE BALL;
THINK BEYOND YOURSELF

GAIL GOODRICH: UCLA VARSITY; 1963–65;
TWO NATIONAL CHAMPIONSHIPS

I came out of high school—LA Poly—as a guard who always thought in terms of having the ball. That's how a guard thinks: "Give me the ball so I can shoot."

Coach Wooden wanted me to think beyond just having the ball because he had decided to install the Press—a full court defense. Of course, when you play defense, you don't have the ball. He was having a little trouble getting me to change my thinking until one day Coach said, "Gail, the game is 40 minutes long. The opponent has the ball approximately half the time. That leaves us 20 minutes with the basketball.

"We have five players. In my system balance is important, so each player should handle the ball about the same amount of time. That means you will have the basketball for approximately four minutes per game. Gail, what are you going to do for the team during those other 35 minutes when you do not have the ball?"

It only took him about 15 seconds, but he dramatically broadened my understanding of the role I needed to play on the team. Coach used a variety of ways to teach what he wanted you to learn. Sometimes during practice he would have the guards switch positions with the forwards—have us do the other guy's job. He wanted everybody to understand the requirements of the player in the other positions. Coach Wooden wanted the guard to appreciate the challenges a forward faced and the forward to appreciate what a guard had to deal with.

He worked very hard to figure out ways to have us think like a team, to work as a unit, not every man out for himself.

I chose UCLA because of how he conducted practices (I had watched the Bruins at the Men's Gym while I was in high school). I was so impressed by his control of the practice, totally in charge.

He had his 3×5 cards and notes and was always looking at the clock to stay on time. He went from one drill to another and then another and another—complete organization; no fooling around, no lulls. He was a master of using time efficiently. Coach could tell you exactly what he had done in practice on that same day 10 years earlier at 4:35 p.m.

He believed that winning is a result of process, and he was a master of the process, of getting us to focus on what we were doing rather than the final score. One drill he had was to run a play over and over at full speed, but he wouldn't let us shoot the ball. He made us concentrate on what happened before the shot was taken, what happened to make it possible. He made us focus on execution. He built teams that knew how to execute.

You knew you were in trouble when you heard him say, "Goodness gracious, sakes alive!" Big trouble. You knew the hammer was heading your way when you heard that. The hammer was the bench, or worse, the shower. Many times he wouldn't exactly tell you what you couldn't do, but he worked things so that it was hard to do them.

Every year during football season there was a Cal Weekend up at Berkeley when the Bruins played the Bears. Coach didn't want his players going up there because it was a big party weekend. But instead of telling us we couldn't go, he just moved practice on Friday back to 6 p.m. Then he kept us late and worked us so hard that nobody had the time or energy to drive all night to get there.

But one year John Galbraith and I decided to fly up for Cal Weekend. I was a Beta Theta Pi and had a couple of beers at the fraternity party on Saturday night after the game. Somehow, Coach Wooden found out not only that I went up to Berkeley but that I'd had a few beers.

Monday morning I got a call that he wanted to see me in his office. "Did you have fun this weekend?" he asked. I nodded. "You know, Gail, if I ever see you drinking, you're gone." I nodded, but I was in shock. "How does he know? How did he find out?" I was thinking.

"Now, you've got a very good year coming up. You don't want to jeopardize that, do you? You don't want to hurt the team, do you?" I answered, "No, Coach. I don't want to hurt the team."

"Good. I'll see you at practice."

The thing was, he wouldn't try and catch you doing something wrong like having a beer. That wasn't his style. He wanted you to assume responsibility for your actions, to have self-control. The whole point of that conversation on Monday was to make me think about what choices I was making. And I did.

He always talked about balance: body balance, scoring balance, team balance, and most of all, mental and emotional balance. Your feet have to be in balance. Your body has to be in balance over your feet. Your head needs to be in balance with your body and your arms. He said if you're not in balance, you'll eventually fall over, and he meant it in more ways than one.

I came to see balance as one of the keys to success, not only in basketball, but in life. When things get out of balance, it's generally not good. Everything needs balance. That one word he kept drilling at us—balance—has stuck with me, became important in how I try to do things.

He never talked about winning, even in the locker room just before the first national championship game against Duke. He calmly went through our game plan and said if we played a good 94-foot game, meaning execution of the Press at one end of the court and good play making at the other end, we'd be able to come back in the locker room afterward with our heads held high. Never mentioned winning a championship or winning the game.

But then, just before we went out on the court, he asked us, "Does anybody here remember who was the runner-up in last year's national championship?"

Nobody raised his hand. That's as close as he ever got to a pep talk.

DETAILS ON
THE FIRST DAY

LYNN SHACKLEFORD: UCLA VARSITY, 1967–69;
THREE NATIONAL CHAMPIONSHIPS

The very first team meeting I ever attended at UCLA was a shock. Sitting next to me was another freshman—the guy who had been the most coveted high school player in America, Kareem Abdul-Jabbar (Lewis Alcindor, Jr.).

Scattered around us were our freshman teammates—some of the best in the country—as well as the returning members of UCLA's varsity team that had won the NCAA national championship several months earlier—Edgar Lacey, Kenny Washington, Doug McIntosh, Fred Goss, Mike Lynn, and others.

There was a lot of energy and talent in that room waiting for the arrival of Coach Wooden and his words of wisdom. Pretty soon he walked in and went directly to the front of the classroom in which we had gathered. Finally, the big moment had arrived, my first experience as a member of a UCLA team—reigning national champions!—coached by the famous John Wooden.

He looked at us for a moment and began his remarks. And that's what was shocking: "Gentlemen," he said, "Welcome. Let's get down to business. I want to remind each one of you of a few important rules we have here at UCLA.

Number one: Keep your fingernails trimmed. Number two: Keep your hair short. Number three: Keep your jersey tucked into your trunks at all times." He looked around the room for a moment and then added solemnly: "Am I clear?"

I wondered, "Is he making a joke?" But there was no laughter, not even smiles, from any of the varsity players. They knew better. Nevertheless, I couldn't understand why he was wasting his time on stuff like that.

As the months—eventually years (and three more national championships)—went by, I came to recognize that "stuff like that" was part of the genius in his leadership. There was logic to every move. Details of fingernails, hair, and jerseys led to details of running plays, handling the ball, and everything else—hundreds of small things done right.

Everything was related to everything else; nothing was left to chance; it all had to be done well. Sloppiness was not allowed in anything, not in passing, shooting, or trimming your fingernails and tucking in your jersey.

Coach Wooden taught that great things can only be accomplished by doing the little things right. Doing things right became a habit with us.

He kept it simple. What's more simple than short hair? What's more simple than squaring up for a shot? All these simple little things added up—one at a time—to an enormous amount of information that he presented in a plain and direct way, bit by bit. Ultimately, he and the team put it all together in practice and then in games.

To accomplish this, he thought out his lesson plan for each day's practice with great precision. He knew what he wanted to accomplish and how to do it. Part of his effectiveness may have come from the fact that he has a master's degree in English. He could say in one short sentence what it took others a long time to get out. He could communicate so much so fast—no wasted words, no beating around the bush.

Coach Wooden's practices were very businesslike and his presence very strong. There were times when he got to a level of sternness mixed with some anger that was nothing to fool with. There was never any screaming or yelling, but his intensity was something else. Especially when he thought we weren't giving it our best effort—watch out then.

During a game against Cal (University of California, Berkeley), we went to the locker room at halftime with a lead, but he was very unhappy. The score didn't matter. He felt that we weren't playing with intensity. And he gave us a tongue-lashing that I still remember well. And he did so without screaming or shouting.

The fact that we were ahead was incidental. What mattered to him was that we weren't playing to our potential. And, it worked the other way too. If the score was going against us, but we were giving it our best effort, he wouldn't get upset. Instead, Coach would very calmly instruct us on changes that should be made.

In 1968, number-one-ranked UCLA played number-two-ranked Houston in the Astrodome. It was called the

Game of the Century. The Cougars were undefeated on the year, and UCLA had a 47-game winning streak going.

It was the first regular-season game ever seen on national television, the first ever played in the Astrodome, and the first to have attendance of over 50,000. It was a big deal. Nobody had ever seen anything like it before in college basketball.

UCLA lost in the final seconds, 71–69, and our 47-game winning streak came to an end. After the game, in the locker room, all the Bruins were very interested to see Coach Wooden's reaction. As UCLA players, we had never seen him lose a single game. Suddenly, he had lost, and it was a big game. How would he react?

When Coach walked into the locker room after losing the Game of the Century, he was very even keeled. There was even a slight smile on his face. He told us, "It's not the end of the world. We'll do better next time." He was pleased with our effort. The score was secondary; having our winning streak snapped was not his concern. Our effort on the court had been total. That made him happy.

In 1967, UCLA played in the finals of the NCAA tournament in Louisville. We hadn't lost a game all season. Just before we went on the court to play Dayton for the national championship, the whole team sat in the locker room for Coach Wooden's pregame talk. Four of the starters were first-year varsity players who were about to face their first national championship game in a few minutes—Kareem, Lucius Allen, Kenny Heitz, and me.

Coach Wooden walked up to the chalkboard and began to diagram something, maybe a new play or defensive tactic. But it wasn't. Coach was diagramming where we should stand during the national anthem! He then spoke about our conduct following the game. The day before, players on another team had gotten rowdy, and he cautioned us about behaving badly. He never mentioned anything about the opponent we were going to play for the national championship; no plays, no specifics of the game. None of that.

What this was about, of course, was his belief that by game time his teaching was complete; if he hadn't taught us what we needed to know by then, it was too late.

Of course, he *had* taught us what we needed to know. And it started on the very first day when he walked to the front of the class and said to the freshman and returning varsity players, "Gentlemen, let's get right down to business." And then he told us about fingernails, short hair, and tucking in jerseys.

It's still a little shocking when I think about it.

FLEXIBILITY IN
ENFORCING RULES

BILL HICKS: UCLA VARSITY, 1960–62

One of our top players—maybe our best—got upset about something during practice one day and stormed off the court. This put Coach Wooden in an awkward position because he didn't want to lose the guy. We didn't exactly have a lot of talent to spare.

Coach solved the problem by telling the player who had blown up and walked off the court that he was suspended. However, he then informed the suspended player that our whole team would be allowed to vote on whether or not to let him return. This allowed everybody to save face. It also empowered the team, because it felt like we got in on the decision. Of course, we voted to let him back.

Coach had solved his problem, disciplined the player, and strengthened our team all at the same time. This was typical of his leadership—very innovative.

He treated all the players the same—no favorites—but said he was only human and would probably like some of us more than others. However, he promised to be absolutely fair in his evaluation of us as players. Coach Wooden wanted us to know that there would be no favoritism on his part. We all had an equal chance.

Coach Wooden always had a passion for the little things. He wanted us to tie our shoes the correct way, pivot the correct way. There was a correct way to do everything, and he wanted us to know how.

So he taught us how.

THE POWER OF POTENTIAL

DOUG MCINTOSH: UCLA VARSITY, 1964–66;
TWO NATIONAL CHAMPIONSHIPS

"You can always do more than you think you can." That's the biggest thing I got from Coach Wooden's teaching. There's always more inside if you're willing to work hard enough to bring it out.

Most of the time we don't recognize we have great potential inside. Coach brought out the potential in people. He taught mental readiness: "Be ready and your chance may come. If you're not ready, it may not come again."

Thus, he made me see that there are no *small* opportunities. Every opportunity is big. If you play for only two minutes, make it the best two minutes possible. That's your opportunity, whether in basketball or in life. Be ready; make the most of it. It may not come again.

In 1964 I was on the UCLA bench at the start of 29 consecutive games. The thirtieth game was against Duke for the national championship. When it started, I was on the bench just like the previous 29 games. And I was ready. Everybody on Coach Wooden's bench was ready.

Five minutes into the championship game, Coach gave me an opportunity. I went in at center, replacing Fred Slaughter, who'd gotten off to a slow start. I stayed in until the game was decided and UCLA had won its first national championship.

The next year, 1965, UCLA played Michigan in the championship game. This time I wasn't on the bench. I was a starter, and I played the best 10 minutes of basketball I'd ever played—running up and down the court blocking shots and getting rebounds. Then Coach took me out for a breather and put in Mike Lynn.

Mike played out of his mind—brilliantly. I spent most of the rest of the game on the bench. Mike was ready when his opportunity came, just as I had been the previous year. Either way was fine with me, if it was good for the team.

The year before, Fred Slaughter was OK with me coming in and replacing him. Fred also believed that what was best for the team was best for him.

Where'd we get that concept? Coach Wooden. He taught that across the board to everybody. There's always resentment by some guys who want more playing time, a bigger role, but Coach was very effective in getting people to understand that the team's interests came first, that doing what was best for the team—even if it meant sitting on the bench—was best for us. Now that's a tough lesson to teach. But he did it.

At UCLA we had five guys on the court playing basketball and seven guys on the sidelines forming a cheerleading squad. When I was on the bench, I was a cheerleader, and I felt that it mattered; I needed to be a great cheerleader, because it could help our team.

In 1966, after UCLA won two consecutive national championships, many picked the Bruins to win a third. We didn't, mainly because of injuries. Through it all, Coach Wooden wasn't any different from the year before, when UCLA won a championship, and the year before that, when UCLA won its first title.

He didn't turn into a raving maniac when we started losing games. His demeanor was about the same, championship season or not. No "woe is me"; never a word about bad breaks and injuries.

He built great teams in practice. He was a "practice coach," and he conducted practices at a very high level. How you practice is how you play is what he believed.

He was strict, but there was no sense of fear of him by players. We knew there was nothing personal in his criticism or comments. What he did was always for the common good and welfare of the team. We all knew that and wanted the same.

He taught that discipline is the mark of a good team. And Coach Wooden was disciplined. And part of that meant keeping emotions under control.

I don't know that there was a "secret" to his success. It was just those three things he stressed: fundamentals, condition, and team spirit.

The drills he ran at UCLA were mostly the same drills I had run back in high school—the very same drills. Coach Wooden just did them more repetitively and with more speed and precision. He just demanded a higher level of execution when it came to fundamentals. There was no secret formula.

He was very intense, but not to the point of screaming or pulling out his hair. Coach was dignified and didn't let his emotions show very much. But we all knew what was going on in his mind.

He kept those emotions under control, but sometimes it was right on the edge. The maddest I ever saw him was against Oregon State, when I went up high for a basket and my legs got cut out from under me. I hit the floor and was knocked unconscious. When I woke up, I saw Coach standing there absolutely livid and demanding that the referee throw out the Oregon State player for the cheap shot.

And he wouldn't tolerate cheap shots by us either—no dirty play. If one of his players threw an elbow in anger, he'd pull you and put you on the bench. Then, when it was convenient, he'd let you have it real good.

He was more upset that we'd lost our temper than anything else. He absolutely wanted emotions to be controlled. If you lost it out there, he'd make you pay a price. He knew that when you lost it—when emotions took over—your performance suffered, your potential was locked inside. He wanted that potential out where it could help the team.

BE WILLING TO CHANGE

GARY CUNNINGHAM: UCLA VARSITY, 1960–62;
ASSISTANT COACH, 1966–75;
SIX NATIONAL CHAMPIONSHIPS

Coach Wooden was strongly opposed, in principle, to the 3–2 zone defense—a half-court defensive system. Nevertheless, Denny Crum and I, assistant coaches, thought it could be very effective for the Bruins to install it. We recommended that he make the change.

Keep in mind, at this point Coach Wooden's teams had just won five national championships in six years. He could easily have told us, "If it ain't broke, don't fix it." However, Coach was always willing to listen, to evaluate new ideas, to seek ways to improve our team. He was never satisfied—never satisfied.

So, despite the fact that UCLA was undefeated at that point in the season, 20–0, Denny and I convinced him to install the 3–2 zone defense for a series up at Oregon.

UCLA won the first game against the University of Oregon, 75–58, but the next night, using the same 3–2 zone against Oregon State, we got beaten, 78–65, and it was apparent the new system wasn't all we thought it might be.

That was the last time we brought up the 3–2 zone defense.

But Coach Wooden had listened and given it—and us— a chance. He wasn't afraid to make a change. And when it didn't work, there were no recriminations. He moved on without making us feel we had led him down the wrong path.

He did not want "yes-men" around him. We were encouraged to argue our points, knowing he'd come back at us strong with his own opinions. That was his way of testing how much we believed in what we were telling him and how much we knew about it.

For example, we'd debate the pivot—what was the best way to do it—for 45 minutes during a morning meeting. But he listened with an open mind, let us contribute—insisted on it. During those meetings, we didn't just sit and take notes. He wanted interaction, ideas back and forth. And he got it. And, of course, he taught us to pay attention and teach details—the little things, like the correct way to pivot.

Those little things that got a lot of attention are one of the secrets to his great strength, namely, organization. We planned practices down to the exact minute.

He had us address the team before games and made sure the assistant coaches talked to the players in the huddle during time-outs. He was very inclusive and gave us both authority and respect.

When we fouled up, he never criticized us in front of the team, nor would he allow the players to challenge us. He insisted on having them address us as Coach Cunningham or Coach Crum rather than by a nickname or informally as Gary or Denny.

In the locker room talks, there was no yelling, no pounding on the wall. It was focused and intense, and always at the end he'd say: "Now go out there and do your best so you can come back in here with your heads up. Let's make sure you can do that."

He was very efficient in his teaching and kept it simple—broke it down into parts, taught each part, then built the whole back up. Always he used the laws of learning: explanation, demonstration, imitation, and repetition. Lots of repetition. You can't believe the repetition.

Coach Wooden didn't believe in lengthy discussions. He was very succinct, clear, substantive. When I first started with him as an assistant, if I took more than 10 seconds to say something during practice, he'd say, "C'mon, let's get going. C'mon." Not rude, just a great sense of urgency.

I learned to keep it short and say it right. Every word counted, because he believed every minute mattered.

The way he conducted himself embodied the Pyramid. It wasn't until later that I realized he was teaching the Pyramid all the time with the model of his behavior.

Teamwork was so important. He kept saying that it doesn't matter who gets credit. If we play together as a team, each player doing his job, we'll like the results. We'll all get credit.

He was prepared, and he got us prepared. People can see when you're not prepared. UCLA was always prepared.

Coach Wooden was an intense competitor and loved to win. But, win or lose, it was always on an even keel. He didn't want us to get too excited about winning, even if it was a national championship.

He was a strong disciplinarian, but he demanded discipline in a very controlled way. "Goodness gracious sakes" was real angry for him. He was a master at analyzing personalities. Player A might just need an explanation. Player B might need some push. He knew what everybody needed to learn his lessons, and he supplied it.

Like with Sidney Wicks. Sidney loved the practices, so the worst possible thing he could do to Sidney was say, "Sidney, you're not with it today. Take a shower." No screaming, yelling. That was it, "Take a shower."

He kept it simple—but intense; not emotional, just very intense.

WIN, WIN, WIN?
NO, NO, NO.

DAVE MEYERS: UCLA VARSITY; 1973–75;
TWO NATIONAL CHAMPIONSHIPS

I retired from the pros when I was 26 after being drafted by Los Angeles as part of a trade that sent me to Milwaukee. On the first day of practice there, I think I heard the "F" word 150 times. Quite a change from Coach Wooden. But that wasn't the only change—just the most inconsequential.

As a pro, absolutely nothing else mattered but winning. If you missed a shot or made a mistake, you were made to feel so bad about it because all eyes were on the scoreboard. Winning was all that mattered and all anybody talked about: "We've gotta win this game," or "We shoulda won that game," or "How can we win the next game?" Win. Win. Win.

Coach Wooden didn't talk about winning—ever. His message was to give the game the best you've got. "That's the goal," he would tell us. "Do that and you should be happy. If enough of you do it, our team will be a success." He teaches this, he believes it, and he taught me to believe it.

Winning was not mentioned, ever—only the effort, the preparation, doing what it takes to bring out our best in practice and games. Let winning take care of itself.

When I was a senior playing forward at UCLA, none of the experts really thought we'd do much. The Walton Gang—Bill Walton, Keith Wilkes, and others—had just graduated after winning two national championships and extending a streak that got up to 88 straight victories before a loss to Notre Dame. I was the only returning starter on the 1974–1975 Bruins.

Coach went to work with us—fundamentals, drills, teamwork, self-sacrifice. Play hard, don't get down, wait for your chance, try to improve each day. Don't worry about the scoreboard. Never a single word about winning. We won the national championship that year.

At the time I didn't quite see it, but his behavior was basically the Pyramid of Success—hard work, energy and enthusiasm, self-control, and the rest of it. That's him. And he taught it by being himself.

In fact, I kind of thought of him as a professor. When I interviewed with him while I was in high school at Sonora, California, I remember, his office at UCLA was full of books, memorabilia, papers, plaques, certificates, lots of stuff. It seemed like the office of an English professor.

On the wall he had pictures of his own coaches—"Piggy" Lambert at Purdue, Glenn Curtis at Martinsville High School, and Earl Warriner from his grade school days in Centerton. There was a large drawing of his Pyramid of Success next to them.

Before practice, he'd often be standing there as we walked on to the court: "How's your mother, David? Have you called her?" "You over that cold, Jim?" "How's the math class coming?" He knew us as people. You could tell he cared. And you could tell that he really knew how to teach—just like a professor.

And, in a certain kind of way he was a professor. What he taught was how to win. And he did it without ever once mentioning winning.

THE FICKLE
FINGER OF FATE

KEN WASHINGTON: UCLA VARSITY, 1964–66;
TWO NATIONAL CHAMPIONSHIPS

The great lesson I take from Coach Wooden is this: the best thing you can do in life is your best. You're a winner when you do that, even if you're on the short end of the score.

Too many factors can affect the final results; the fickle finger of fate can suddenly take over. The best talent doesn't always win, but the individual or team that goes out and does their best is a winner. That's his philosophy. It's what he teaches.

We had a perfect season and won the national championship in 1964. We repeated as national champions in 1965. There was no question in my mind that in 1966 we could become the first team in college basketball history to win three championships in a row. Then the fickle finger of fate pointed at us.

Injuries, sickness, and all kinds of stuff were hitting us. We didn't even win our conference title in 1966—we had a 10–4 record and weren't even eligible to play in the NCAA tournament and defend our title.

Through all the misfortune, I never heard a single complaint or excuse from Coach Wooden. He fought hard and kept telling us to keep working, never give up, and do our best. And we did in spite of the fickle finger of fate.

We were winners in 1966 because of that.

In retrospect, I believe it was probably fantastic for me as a person that we didn't win that third consecutive national championship. It showed me what life is really like, what fate can do—why you can't base your success just on results.

Of course, this is what I had been taught by my coach. More than anyone I've ever known, he comes closest to practicing what he preaches. He was so consistent in what he said and did in both principles and standards. In fact, I began to think it was normal behavior in a leader. But it's not normal. Holding to those high standards and principles is rare out in the world.

At the end of my four years at UCLA, I still needed additional credits to graduate. Coach Wooden was all over me to make sure I came back for that fifth year to earn my degree in Economics.

Even though my playing days were over at UCLA, he cared a great deal about my welfare. "This is very important for you, Kenneth. Let's get that diploma." And he kept checking in on me during the year to make sure I got it. And I did.

Coach Wooden didn't teach character; he nurtured it. He chose individuals to be on the team based on talent, of course, but not talent alone. He wanted a certain kind of individual—the team player, a person with integrity and values.

Then he nurtured those values just like he nurtured your talent as an athlete. Honesty, being unselfish, caring about your teammates, a good work ethic, all these things were stressed constantly.

Along with this, he would never degrade, abuse, or humiliate individuals, even though he had the power to do it. After all, he was the boss. But he gave respect even when discipline was doled out.

Coach is a master psychologist who understands the differences in people. Certain things he insisted on, like no swearing, being on time, no showboating, all of that. But when it came to working with us, he treated everybody as an individual, approached each of us in a way that worked.

Jack Hirsch, for example, was a free spirit, very flippant, and the only guy on the team who addressed Coach Wooden as John. Coach understood that it was not being done in a disrespectful manner and let him do it. Coach knew Jack wasn't crossing the line. It was just Jack being Jack.

When he crossed the line, however, there was a price to pay. One day we were eating dinner at the training table and Jack got up and said, "I can't eat this slop." Coach very calmly, but firmly, suspended Jack—told him not to come back until he could apologize as well as eat what all the other players were eating.

Coach understood the disrespect that was carried in Jack's remarks about our food. Disrespect by anyone for anyone was simply not allowed.

Now, where Jack came from, maybe our training table food didn't taste good. As far I was concerned, it was fine. Coach understood he could not let Jack say what he said. It was not acceptable, disrespectful. Jack remained off the team until he changed his attitude and apologized.

Two weeks later Jack was back at the training table, not exactly wolfing it down, but not complaining either.

Athletics is like life. Sometime you can do everything right and still lose. It's all a journey. You do your best, and then you have to let it go. Lots of people preach that, but come crunch time—oops, not so easy to do. Coach practiced what he preached. Even when the fickle finger of fate took over.

EMOTIONS CAN MAKE
YOU VULNERABLE

Kareem Abdul-Jabbar
(Lewis Alcindor, Jr.)
UCLA varsity, 1967–69
three national championships

His approach was *very* dispassionate. He taught that big emotions were an extra burden that we didn't need to contend with. Coach Wooden felt that if you needed all kinds of emotion to do your job, then you were vulnerable. There was never any "You gotta go out and kill these guys" talk from Coach Wooden to get us keyed up. He'd say, "I want you to go out there and do your best the way we practiced it." There was never any speech telling us to go out and "win this game!" to get us charged up, no [emotional] juice he tried to put in the mix. We understood that if we played up to the standard he had set in practice, we'd probably win. If not, if we lost, he took the blame and tried to fix it the next practice. He was very focused, very intense. Always, always with his emotions under control.

WORK HARD
OR LEAVE

DAVE MEYERS
UCLA VARSITY, 1973–75

He loved sharpness. If Coach Wooden didn't see it in practice, that intensity of attention and execution—the *effort*—he might say very coldly, "O.K., we're through today. You didn't come here to work." Marques Johnson or one of us would say, "No, no, no. We'll get it going. C'mon, we'll get it going." Almost pleading with him to give us another chance to work harder.

Maybe his Midwestern upbringing, that lifestyle, put a love of hard work into him. Coach Wooden loved hard work. He wanted to see it from the players. If not, no yelling or screaming, he'd just threaten to end practice. And he wasn't afraid to follow through on the threat.

I LEARN WHO'S THE STAR

ANDRE McCARTER
UCLA VARSITY, 1974–76

As a high school player in South Philly at Overbrook High School, I won every honor you could get: MVP, Player of the Year, High School All-American as a junior and senior, and lots of attention. Colleges were promising me things you couldn't believe.

Then I talked to Coach Wooden on a trip to California. He was strictly no frills. He didn't promise me I'd start or anything like that. He promised me only one thing, specifically, that I'd get a very good education with my athletic scholarship—that and a $20 laundry expense.

If I wanted to be "the star," I knew I had to go someplace else. At UCLA the star was Coach Wooden's team. That was his system. The team was the star.

DETAILED PREPARATION
AND TRAINING

RAY REGAN
SOUTH BEND CENTRAL HIGH SCHOOL VARSITY,
1938–39; LAWYER

Coach Wooden always carried a No. 2 yellow pencil. It seemed like the only time he didn't have his No. 2 yellow pencil in his hand was when he was holding a basketball.

He wrote everything down, kept track of all kinds of stuff during practice and games. Coach Wooden was amazing when it came to keeping records of our statistics and then training us to improve on them. I still remember that No. 2 yellow pencil.

I also remember we used to have a showboat on our team, a player who was always yelling for the ball, and then once he got it would keep it until he took a shot. Then he'd start yelling for the ball again.

One day, during a five-on-five scrimmage, Coach Wooden decided to teach the showboat a lesson about teamwork. Coach took the four of us aside and said to pass the basketball to our teammate the ball hog. Then we were told to run immediately to the middle of the court, all four of us, sit down, and let the showboat play the other team all by himself.

It was Coach's way of showing this guy that everybody helps everybody or nothing gets done.

After that little lesson in sharing, the showboat started passing more often. It was a great way of teaching a lesson that is hard for some people to learn. And Coach did it many different ways.

His strength was in teaching fundamentals through hard work. Nobody raced to the showers when practice was over. Most of us just sat on the bench in the locker room completely whipped—exhausted. Occasionally, the custodian would even come by and plead with us, "C'mon, guys, I want to get home for dinner. Take your showers!" Coach worked us hard.

We used to pray for the game to come because practices were so demanding. But it paid off. In 1939 we were 18–2 overall and favored to win the Indiana State High School tournament. Unfortunately, it wasn't meant to be. Just before the Sectionals began, the flu hit everybody on our team. We didn't stand a chance. The Bears lost to our archrivals Mishawaka.

Afterward, Coach Wooden said he was proud of us, how we gave it everything we had, that we could hold our heads high. There was disappointment in our locker room, but I don't believe any player felt like a loser. We had given it our best.

Beyond teaching fundamentals, Coach Wooden was aiming at something else.

When the players got rambunctious, a little out of hand, started acting like teenagers, he'd stop *everything* and say very strongly, "Fellas, I want you to become men, not just beat somebody in basketball." And he really meant it. His teaching went beyond just trying to win.

Before games he told us to do our best, never harbor ill feelings if we lost, never denigrate our opponent, and, if they played well, to congratulate them. And, of course, no profanity.

His morality—that basic decency he has—affected me deeply. He was a gentle man who was a very strong coach.

I came away from him with a feeling of wanting to do my best in whatever I took on. We were prepared and trained well. And not just for basketball.

A GENIUS FOR KNOWING WHAT MAKES YOU TICK

KEITH ERICKSON
UCLA VARSITY, 1963–65,
TWO NATIONAL CHAMPIONSHIPS

What made Coach Wooden so effective as a leader was his ability to work with every type of person—different temperaments, personalities, styles, and all the rest. He knew how to get them to do it his way, and this included people who were total opposites.

UCLA's Gail Goodrich and Walt Hazzard were the greatest combination of guards in the history of college basketball; the best twosome ever, in my opinion. But they were totally different guys.

With Gail, Coach would come up and sort of cajole him, put his arm around him and low-key it—offer a quiet suggestion, a little compliment. Then he'd give him a pat on the back and walk away. He knew that Gail wouldn't react to sharp criticism; it would hurt his play.

Coach knew a stronger approach worked with Walt. There was no mincing words. He'd say very firmly, "Walt, if you do that again, you're out of here." And if Walt did it again, he'd hear Coach say, "O.K., that's it. Take a shower." Not with any anger, just very stern.

He was so smart in administering discipline, avoiding backing himself into a corner. So with Walt, he'd say, "If you do that *again*. . . ." He didn't want Walt taking a shower before practice was concluded, so he gave him a chance or two to correct the problem. Walt knew he could get away with a little, but not much.

Coach treated each one of us the way we needed to be treated, the way that worked best for each person. Coach believed or understood that no two of us were alike. His understanding of people and how to work with each player individually was evident in practice every day. With me there was no cajoling. He knew a sharp remark would have a positive effect. And I got 'em.

Always Coach Wooden emphasized playing together as a team, a unit, a single group. That was all-important, everything.

Our team in 1964—the one that won a national championship—wasn't buddy-buddy off the court, but on the court you'd think we loved each other because there was such camaraderie and selflessness.

Coach Wooden acted as a scoutmaster, den mother, surrogate parent, second father, drill sergeant—and a man. He was tough as nails, and yet he showed this great love for his wife and kids—his family. To have a coach who was so tough—strong—who loved his wife so much . . . well, it affected my thinking of him. It really brought out respect. He got this great respect from us. And he gave it back.

We got treated like part of the family. Kenny Washington, whose own family lived on the other side of the country, was invited over to the Woodens for holiday dinners so he wouldn't be alone. And there were others.

John Wooden knew what worked for each one of us. He understood what made us tick.

IT'S WHAT YOU LEARN
AFTER YOU KNOW IT ALL
THAT COUNTS

BILL WALTON
UCLA VARSITY, 1972–74,
TWO NATIONAL CHAMPIONSHIPS

I stopped listening to Coach Wooden in my senior year, 1974. All the things that made us a great team as sophomores and juniors evaporated like dust in the wind. It was after this depressing meltdown [UCLA's 88-game winning streak was broken, and the team lost in the semifinals of the Final Four, which ended the winning streak of seven consecutive championships] that Coach penned his famous maxim, "It's what you learn after you know it all that counts." This prophetic lesson of life was directed specifically to me. I now have the original sitting as the centerpiece on my desk, personally signed by the master teacher himself. And I can see him this very moment slowly shaking his head with that sad, disappointed look on his face—like a father who's been let down.

ABOUT STEVE JAMISON

*Steve Jamison understands
what I did and why I did it. Equally important,
he has a terrific ability to articulate both.*
—JOHN WOODEN

Steve Jamison is America's foremost author and authority on
the leadership philosophy and methodology created by Coach
John Wooden. For more than a decade, he and Mr. Wooden
have collaborated in bringing the legendary coach's leadership ideas to a vast audience. Together they have authored
five best-selling books, including *Wooden
on Leadership* (McGraw-Hill), *The Essential Wooden* (McGraw-Hill), *My Personal
Best: Life Lessons from an All American
Journey* (McGraw-Hill), and *Wooden: A
Lifetime of Observations and Reflections*
(Contemporary Publishing). Their book
for children, *Inch and Miles: The Journey to Success* (Perfec-
tion Learning), is being read in grade schools across America.

Mr. Jamison is executive producer of the award-winning
PBS presentation, "WOODEN: Values, Victory, and Peace of

Mind" and has appeared with Mr. Wooden at numerous corporate presentations, including Disney Resorts, General Mills, CitiBank, Waste Connections, Inc., and UCLA's Anderson School of Management. He serves as a consultant to the UCLA Anderson School of Management's John Wooden Global Leadership Program and is a popular public speaker.

Additionally, he is executive producer of John Wooden Leadership, a teaching forum dedicated to sharing the leadership philosophy and methodology of Coach Wooden. Mr. Jamison is creative director of CoachWooden.com, the official Web site of John Wooden. For more visit www.Steve Jamison.com

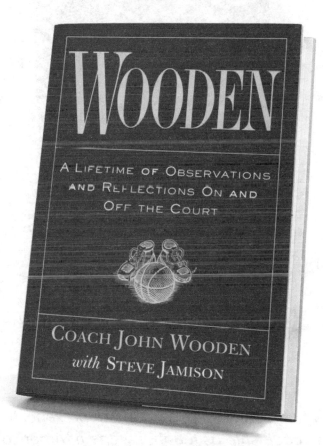

AN INSIDE LOOK

THE ESSENTIAL

Wooden

A Lifetime of Lessons on Leaders and Leadership

JOHN WOODEN
AND STEVE JAMISON

AT THE LEADERSHIP WISDOM OF COACHING LEGEND, JOHN WOODEN

"Coach Wooden's moral authority and brilliant definition of success encompass all of life. How I admire his life's work and concept of what it really means to win!"

—Stephen R. Covey, author, *The 7 Habits of Highly Successful People* and *The 8th Habit: From Effectiveness to Greatness*

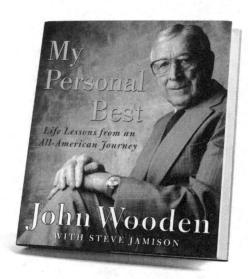
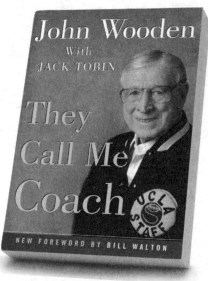